BLISSFUL BEGINNINGS

embroidered blankets to cherish

EXECUTIVE EDITOR	Anna Scott
EDITOR	Jessica Marshallsay
CREATIVE DIRECTOR	Fiona Fagan
EDITORIAL TEAM	Ellaine Bronsert, Heidi Reid
ILLUSTRATIONS & DIAGRAMS	Kathleen Barac
PATTERN DESIGN	Kathleen Barac
GRAPHIC DESIGN	Linda Dunlop, Lynton Grandison
PHOTOGRAPHY	ADP

Distribution Enquiries
CB PUBLICATIONS
916 South Road, Edwardstown
South Australia 5039, Australia
Phone: +61 8 8293 8600
Fax: +61 8 8293 8733
Email: marketing@countrybumpkin.com.au
Website: www.countrybumpkin.com.au

Published in Australia by
CB PUBLICATIONS
Printed and bound in China

Blissful Beginnings: Embroidered blankets to cherish
ISBN 9780980876734
Copyright © Buckleboo Belle Pty Ltd Australia, 2012

National Library of Australia Cataloguing-in-Publication entry
Blissful Beginnings: Embroidered blankets to cherish
Executive editor: Anna Scott; editor: Jessica Marshallsay
9780980876734 (pbk.)
Embroidery. Blankets. Embroidery--Patterns
746.440437

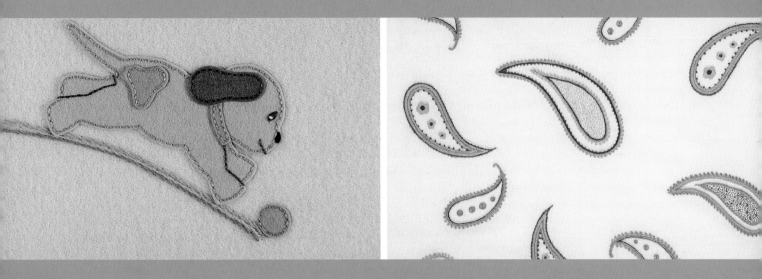

CONTENTS

WELCOME

The arrival of a new baby is a joyous occasion. What better way to welcome him or her than with a gorgeous embroidered blanket or gift, lovingly hand stitched by you.

From serene florals to cheery nursery rhymes, there are designs to suit every taste. Both beautiful and versatile, within these pages you'll find irresistible blankets, a delicate wrap, a handy shoulder cloth and fun soft toys. Whether you're looking to create a unique welcome gift for a precious newborn, a special birthday blanket for a toddler to snuggle under, or even an elegant throw to display in your living room, you are sure to find a design to capture your heart.

Suitable for both experienced embroiderers and those who have only just picked up a needle, you will find inspiration, clear instructions and many blissful hours of stitching inside this book. We hope you enjoy savouring every page!

Getting started

Preparing the fabric

Laundering

Many fabrics will shrink a little when they are washed for the first time, and dark or bright colours will often contain a bit of excess dye that will come out in the first wash. It is therefore a good idea to launder fabrics before you begin your stitching to avoid any nasty surprises later. Launder your fabric following the manufacturer's care instructions.

HOW MUCH FABRIC?

Many of the fabric measurements provided in this book are exact. It's a good idea to buy a bit extra, especially for the backing fabrics. Once you've laundered it, you can cut it to the required size.

Raw edges

When you handle a cut piece of fabric, the edges will loosen and begin to fray. To prevent this happening, neaten the raw edges with an overlock or machine zigzag stitch, or by hand with an overcast stitch around the edges (*diags 1 & 2*).

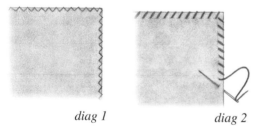

diag 1   *diag 2*

Alternatively, fold each side of the fabric twice to enclose the raw edge and tack in place (*diag 3*).

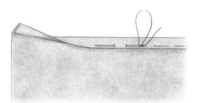

diag 3

Tacking

Tacking is a row of temporary stitches used to hold pieces of fabric together or to mark out placement guides for positioning your embroidery design. Tacking is best worked using a light coloured machine sewing thread (*diag 4*).

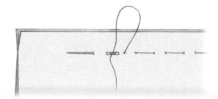

diag 4

WHAT IS THE GRAIN OF THE FABRIC?

The grain is the direction in which the threads of a fabric run.

When cutting fabrics, make sure you cut along the grain, following a fabric thread, to ensure you achieve straight edges (*diag 5*).

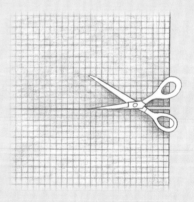

diag 5

WHAT IS THE BIAS?

The bias of a fabric is diagonally across the grain. If you pull the fabric on the bias you will distort the threads and the shape of the piece. It is particularly important to remember not to pull the fabric on the bias when mounting it into a hoop.

Preparing the threads

How to use a looped skein

- Leave the tags on the skein and undo the little paper lock on one tag if it has one.

- Gently pull out the end of the thread from the centre of the skein (*diag 6*).

diag 6

- You can also remove the tags and wind the thread onto a card.

How to use a twisted skein

- Slide the tags off the skein. If there is only one tag, cut it in half.

- Untwist and open the skein, and cut all the threads at one end.

- Fold the bundle in half and slide the tags back onto the threads.

diag 7

- Divide the threads into three even groups (*diag 7*).

- Make a soft plait. The threads can now be pulled out individually near the tags (*diag 8*).

diag 8

HOW LONG IS A LENGTH OF THREAD?

It is best to work with threads no more than 35cm (14"), or the distance from your thumb to your elbow. Longer threads will wear and may easily become tangled.

SEPARATING STRANDS – STRIPPING

When you need to use more than one strand at a time, it is important to separate the strands and then put them back together. This is known as 'stripping' the thread.

- Hold the end of all the strands between your thumb and index finger.

- Ease out a single strand and pull it upwards out of the bundle (*diag 9*). Do not peel it off.

diag 9

- The remaining strands will fall back neatly. Repeat for the required number of strands before re-grouping them and threading them into the needle.

Using a hoop

Whether or not to use a hoop can be a personal choice, and also varies depending on the project. In this book, we have indicated which projects we recommend working in a hoop.

Choose a hoop large enough for the design to fit inside the ring, so that you avoid flattening finished sections of embroidery.

Binding a hoop

Binding the inner ring of the hoop will prevent the fabric from slipping while you stitch. To bind it you can use white cotton tape or bias binding ironed flat.

- Hold the end of the binding and wrap it around the inner ring of the hoop.

- Secure the binding with small back stitches at the edge of the binding.

- Wrap the binding around the hoop, ensuring there are no creases and that the layers of binding overlap.

- When reaching the starting point, cut off the excess binding and secure the end with small back stitches.

How to place fabric in a hoop

- Loosen the tension screw so the two rings slip apart.

- Place the inner ring on a table and position the fabric over the ring.

- Press the outer ring down over the fabric and tighten the screw.

- If you need to tighten the fabric further, make sure you only pull with the grain of the fabric. If you pull the fabric on the bias it will stretch and become distorted.

- Take the fabric out of the hoop when you are not stitching, to avoid leaving a permanent mark.

TO SEW OR NOT TO SEW

Most stitches can be either 'sewn' or 'stabbed'. Always stab the needle through the fabric when working in a hoop, as skimming the needle will distort the fabric (*diag 10*)

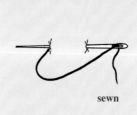

sewn   stabbed

diag 10

SECURING YOUR THREADS
Stitching

This method is quite secure and is suitable for almost any type of embroidery.

- Begin in an area that will be covered by embroidery and close to the starting point for the stitching. Leave a short tail and take two tiny stitches on the back of the fabric, splitting the first stitch (*diag 11*).

diag 11

- Work a few more stitches into the first two to secure the thread firmly. Trim the tail.

- Finish in a similar way with several small back

stitches into the stitches on the wrong side of the fabric, making sure the thread doesn't show on the front.

Weaving

Weaving is suitable only for stitching that will not need washing, as the thread tails can come undone.

- Begin by leaving a 10cm (4") tail of thread hanging on the back of the fabric.

- After working a small part of the embroidery, re-thread the tail and weave it under the stitches on the back. For added strength, make two or more small stitches into the back of the work. Trim the tail.

- Finish in the same way.

Knots

These are easy to use when you have a textured surface, such as thick embroidery, as the small lump from the knot won't show on the front.

- Thread the needle. Hold a short tail of thread along the shaft of the needle with the tail towards the eye.

- Hold the tail and the needle in one hand. With the other hand, wrap the thread around the point of the needle 2–4 times.

- Holding the wraps between your thumb and index finger, pull the needle through the wraps. This creates a neat, consistent knot.

- Finish as for the stitching method.

Finishing your embroidery

Cleaning and pressing

Once the stitching is complete the project will need to be 'finished'. This may involve washing, or if the fabric or threads are not colourfast or washable, you may need to have it dry cleaned.

Wash the work by hand in lukewarm water using a mild detergent. Be careful not to rub the surface of your stitching, as this will cause pilling.

Rinse the work thoroughly in clean water. Roll it up in a clean towel and press as much excess water out as possible, but do not wring it. Dry the piece flat as quickly as possible, away from direct sunlight.

Pressing your embroidery can make a huge difference to the overall finish of the work. Avoid pressing the right side as this will flatten the threads too much.

Fold a towel into a few thicknesses and place it on your ironing board. Place the work, with the embroidery facing down onto the towel, and press the back of the work using a setting appropriate for the fabric. The stitches will sink into the towel and you will be able to press the fabric flat.

When things go wrong

- If you prick your finger and get blood on the fabric, chew a piece of sewing thread or scrap of fabric and use this to dab off the blood. Your saliva removes your own blood.

- If you make a mistake, don't panic! In most cases, small mistakes are not critical and whether or not to unpick is a personal choice. You can decide to leave the imperfect or incorrect stitching as your artistic rendition. On the other hand, if you know it is going to irritate you every time you look at the piece, take the time to correct it.

- If you decide to unpick, unthread the needle and use the eye end to pull the stitches out. Don't attempt to stitch back through the fabric.

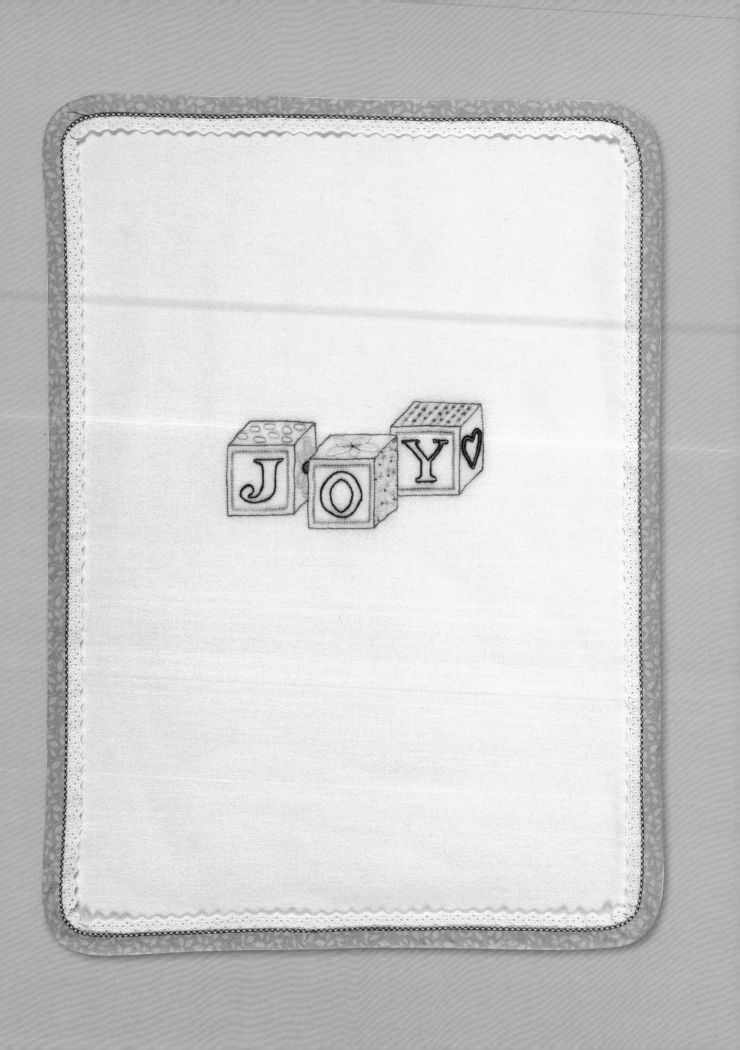

Bundle of Joy

by Anna Scott

There's nothing quite as joyful as the birth of a new baby. Perfect for a boy or girl, this stylish design spells it out to the world on an adorable bassinette blanket to welcome the new arrival.
A perfect weekend project for the busy stitcher.

The finished blanket measures
70cm x 50cm wide (27 ½" x 20").

This Design Uses

Back stitch	French knot
Chain stitch	Running stitch
Cross stitch	Satin stitch
Detached chain	Stem stitch
Fly stitch	Straight stitch

Requirements

Fabric

70cm x 50cm wide (27 ½" x 20") piece of ivory doctor's flannel

70cm x 50cm wide (27 ½" x 20") piece of ivory cotton batiste

50cm x 112cm wide (20" x 44") piece of tan print cotton

Supplies

2.5m (2yd 27") red and white check mini piping

2.5m x 25mm wide (2yd 27" x 1") ivory embroidered Swiss lace edging

Tracing paper

Fine black pen

Fine water-soluble fabric marker

Threads
Cascade House shaded crewel wool

A = 1000/6 warm white

B = 1000/10 stone white

C = 2570/6 dk mocha

D = 3970/10 garnet

E = 7940/2 vy lt grey-green

Needle

No. 5 crewel

Preparation for Embroidery

See the liftout pattern for the embroidery design.

We recommend that you read the complete article and instructions on pages 78–84 relating to this project before you begin.

Preparing the fabric

Fold the doctor's flannel in half lengthwise. Tack along the foldline and unfold. Measure 30cm (12") along the tacked line from the upper edge. Fold the fabric widthwise at this point. Tack along the foldline as before. Unfold.

Transferring the design

Trace the embroidery design and placement marks onto the tracing paper with the pen. Place the tracing over a lightbox or window and tape in place. Position the doctor's flannel over the tracing, aligning the placement marks with the tacked lines. Tape in place. Trace the embroidery design onto the fabric with the water-soluble marker.

Embroidery

Refer to the close-up photograph for colour placement. All embroidery is worked with one strand of wool. Take care not to pull the stitches too tight, as this will pucker and distort the fabric.

Outline the blocks in back stitch with C, keeping the stitches short and even. Change to E and embroider the square on the front of each block in chain stitch. To turn a corner, finish the row along one side with a small anchoring stitch, then emerge inside the last

stitch to continue stitching along the adjacent side. Using D, work the outline of the letter on each block in stem stitch.

J-BLOCK

Embroider the outline of each dot on the top of the block in back stitch with E. Fill the dots with satin stitch using A, keeping the stitches inside the outlines.

Outline the flower petals with two rows of stem stitch using B. Fill the petals with satin stitch using the same thread, working the stitches diagonally across each petal. Stitch the flower centre with 2-wrap French knots, starting with D along the outline and changing to E for the filling.

O-BLOCK

Embroider the star on top of the block with A. Begin each segment with a long straight stitch at the point, then fill with closely worked fly stitches *(diag 1)*.

diag 1

Repeat for the remaining four segments, then work straight stitches to fill any gaps at the centre of the star. Outline the star in back stitch using the same thread to define the shape. Change to C and work five straight stitches to divide the segments, bringing the needle to the front on the outline and to the back through the centre.

Stitch five detached chain petals for each small daisy on the side of the block using B. Work a 2-wrap French knot at the centre of each flower with C, and scatter small fly stitches among the daisies with E for the foliage (diag 2).

Y-BLOCK

Work a row of long running stitches along each line on the top of the block with E. Change to C and work a cross stitch between each running stitch.

Outline the heart in stem stitch with D. Work a second row of stem stitch just inside the first row with E. Stitch the innermost row of stem stitch with D.

Hint

For a blue version of this blanket, replace the red yarn with Cascade House shaded crewel wool no. 9560/10, and use a matching ricrac instead of the embroidered lace edging – **Anna**

Construction

See pages 78 – 84.

diag 2

Bundle of Joy Blocks

By Anna Scott

Whether they're treasured as baby's first toys or nursery decorations, these delightful soft blocks will make a unique gift to cherish and can be whipped up in an afternoon or two.

Each side of the finished blocks measures 6cm (2 ³/₈") square.

This Design Uses

Appliqué
Blanket stitch
Stem stitch

Requirements

Fabric
Selection of coordinating print cottons in tones of ivory, sand and red.
8 x 15cm (6") squares for the embroidered sides
16 x 7cm (2 ³/₄") squares for the remaining sides

Supplies
30cm x 70cm wide (12" x 28") piece of thick wadding
Small piece of appliqué paper
Matching sewing thread
10cm (4") embroidery hoop (optional)
Fine water-soluble fabric marker
Sharp lead pencil
Fine black pen
Tracing paper

Threads & Needle
Stranded cotton
Select four or five colours to match your fabrics. For these blocks, ecru, two shades of red, soft brown and beige were used.
No. 9 crewel needle

Preparation for Embroidery

See the liftout pattern for the embroidery designs and heart template.

We recommend that you read the complete article before you begin.

Preparing the fabric

Cut eight pieces, each 15cm (6") square from different fabrics for the embroidered sides of the blocks.

Transferring the designs

Trace the heart and grainline onto the appliqué paper with the pencil and roughly cut out. Fuse the paper to the wrong side of a piece of red fabric, aligning the grainlines. Cut out along the marked line and remove the backing paper. With the right side facing up, fuse the heart to one of the fabric squares, making sure the grains of the fabrics are aligned.

Trace the remaining embroidery designs and cutting lines onto the tracing paper with the pen. Place one tracing over a lightbox or window and tape in place. Centre a fabric square over a letter, aligning the cutting lines with the straight grain of the fabric, and tape in place. Using the water-soluble marker, trace the letter and cutting lines. Repeat for the remaining letters and fabric squares.

Embroidery

All embroidery is worked with two strands of thread.

LETTERS

For each letter, choose a thread that contrasts nicely with the fabric.

All the letters are embroidered in stem stitch, keeping the stitches short and working from the outline towards the centre.

Work a single row to outline letters on plain or very subtle print fabrics. Embroider two or three close rows for letters worked onto small print fabrics. For letters embroidered onto fabric with large patterns or several colours, you may need to fill the letter completely to make sure it stands out.

HEART

Neaten the outline of the appliqué heart with blanket stitch, using matching stranded cotton.

Construction

See the liftout pattern for the cutting out instructions.

All seam allowances are 6mm (¼") unless otherwise specified. The shaded areas on the following diagrams indicate the right side of the fabric.

1. Preparing the embroidered pieces

Trim the embroidered pieces to size along the marked cutting lines. Remove any visible fabric marker with a damp sponge and leave to dry.

Place the pieces on a well-padded surface with the wrong side facing up and press.

2. Making the blocks

To arrange the pieces for the blocks, lay the first letter of each word in front of you. Place a fabric piece between the 'L' and the 'J', and a second piece after the 'J'. These will become the sides of the block. Choose another two pieces and place above and below the second letter. These will become the top and bottom of the block (*diag 1*).

Lay out the remaining embroidered and plain blocks in the same manner, making sure the fabric square above the second letter is different for each group so that the tops of the blocks vary.

With right sides together and matching raw edges, pin and stitch the first two pieces in the row together, starting and finishing the seam 6mm (¼") from the edges (*diag 2*).

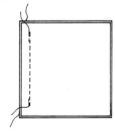

diag 2

Add the third and fourth pieces in a similar manner. Press the seams open. Pin and stitch the pieces for the top and bottom of the block to the remaining sides of the third piece in a similar manner. Press the seams open (*diag 3*).

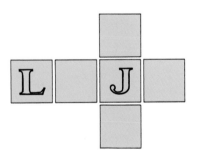

diag 1

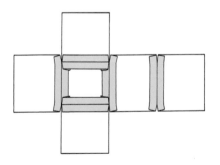

diag 3

Pin and stitch the fourth and first pieces together *(diag 4)*.

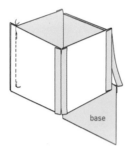

diag 4

Press the seam open. Folding the side pieces out of the way, pin and stitch the top piece to the upper edge of each remaining side piece, completing one side at a time *(diag 5)*.

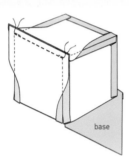

diag 5

Press the seams open. Turn the block to the right side. Press and tack the remaining seam allowances to the wrong side. Repeat for the remaining three blocks.

3. Finishing

Stack ten pieces of wadding into one block, pushing them down firmly. Matching folded edges and corners, pin and handstitch the base of the block in place. Repeat for the remaining three blocks.

Starting at one corner and pinching the seam tightly between your fingers, work blanket stitch over the seam with two strands of coordinating stranded cotton. Repeat along all the remaining seams.

Hint

I prefer to use a hoop when working the stem stitch letters. The hoop will help prevent the lightweight fabric from puckering, especially if you are working multiple rows or filling the letter completely **– Anna**

New Life
by Heather Scott

This eye-catching, contemporary blanket is
a wonderful modern twist on the traditional
Persian motif. With a fresh colour palette
and enticing variety of stitches, this stunning
paisley design is sure to be loved by any
stylish mum or retro chic devotee.

The finished blanket measures
120cm x 75cm wide (47 ¼" x 29 ½").

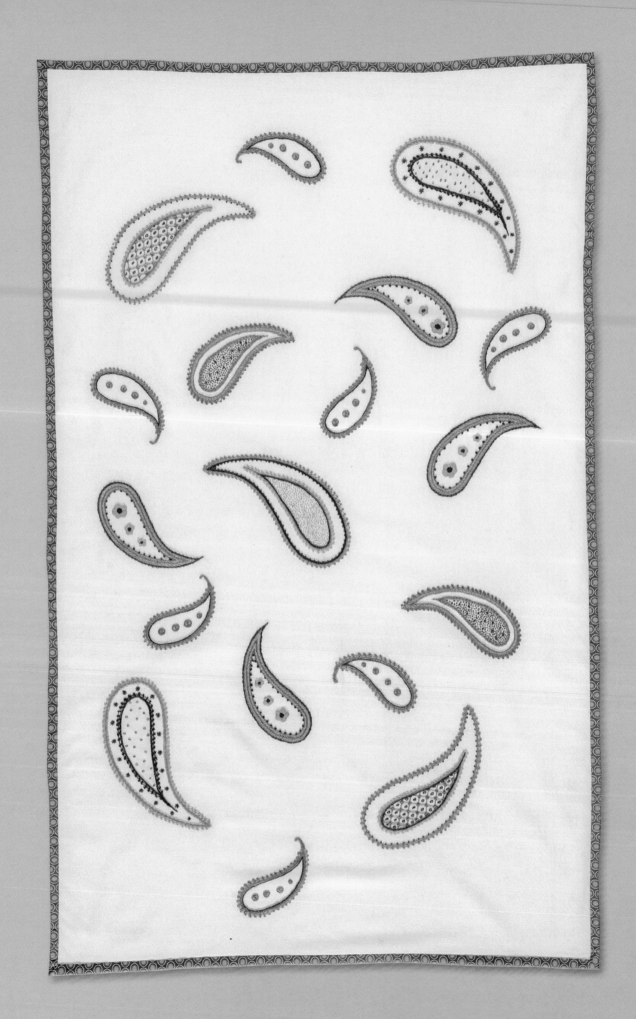

Requirements

Fabric

120cm x 75cm wide (47 ½" x 29 ½") piece of cream doctor's flannel

120cm x 75cm wide (47 ½" x 29 ½") piece of cream cotton broadcloth

50cm x 112cm wide (20" x 44") piece of teal circle print cotton

Supplies

Lightweight card

20cm (8") embroidery hoop

Fine black pen

Fine water-soluble fabric marker

Threads

Appletons crewel wool

A = 243 olive green

B = 251 lt grass green

C = 252 grass green

D = 255 vy dk grass green

E = 352 vy lt grey green

F = 354 grey green

G = 521 ultra lt turquoise

H = 522 vy lt turquoise

I = 542 vy lt early English green

J = 561 ultra lt sky blue

K = 563 lt sky blue

DMC stranded cotton

L = 356 med terracotta

M = 471 vy lt avocado green

N = 518 lt wedgewood

O = 519 vy lt wedgewood

Needles

No. 8 crewel

No. 22 chenille

This Design Uses

Blanket stitch pinwheel	Satin stitch
Chain stitch	Seed stitch
Crested chain stitch	Split stitch
Detached chain	Stem stitch
French knot	Straight stitch
Granitos	Trellis couching
	Twisted chain stitch

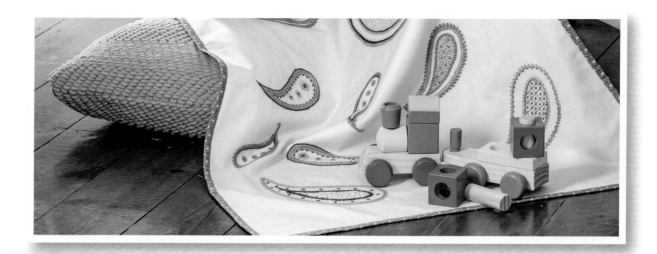

Preparation for Embroidery

See the liftout pattern for the paisley and flower templates.

We recommend that you read the complete article and instructions on page 78–84 relating to this project before you begin.

Transferring the design

Using a lightbox or window, trace five large, six medium and seven small paisley shapes, including markings, onto the lightweight card with the black pen. Cut out each shape and use a large needle to pierce a hole at the marked positions for the spots and flowers on the small and medium paisley shapes. Trace and cut out the three flower templates in the same manner. Pierce a hole at the centre of each flower.

Lay the flannel onto a flat surface. Using the photograph on page 22 as a guide, position and pin the paisley templates in place. Trace around the outline of each shape using the water-soluble fabric marker. On the small shapes, mark the position for the centre of the blanket stitch pinwheels through the hole in the card. Mark the position for the flowers on four of the medium paisley shapes in the same manner.

Unpin and remove the templates. Using a circle template or drawing freehand, mark the outline of the pinwheels, ensuring that the three large spots are 1cm (3/8") in diameter, and the small spot is 7mm (5/16").

On the large shapes, measure and mark with the fabric marker, 2cm (3/4") in from the outline with a dot at regular intervals. Join the dots to form the inner shape *(diag 1)*.

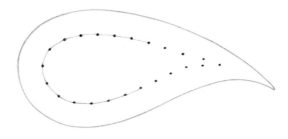

diag 1

On the two speckled medium paisley shapes, measure 1cm (3/8") in from the outline and mark with a dot at regular intervals. Join the dots to form the inner shape in the same manner as before. On the four remaining medium shapes, position the flower templates so the flower centres are aligned with the marked points. Trace around the outline of each flower.

Embroidery

Refer to the close-up photograph for colour placement.

Use the chenille needle for all wool embroidery and the crewel needle for all cotton embroidery.

All embroidery is worked with one strand unless otherwise specified. The trellis couching is worked in the hoop.

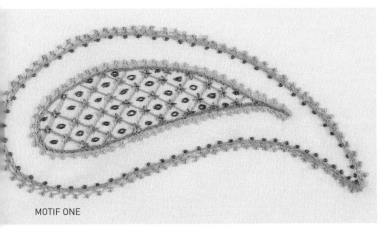

MOTIF ONE

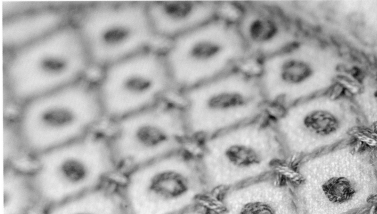

LARGE PAISLEY MOTIFS

Using one strand of H, outline each large paisley with stem stitch.

MOTIF ONE

Two of the larger paisleys at the corners are embroidered in this manner. Using H, work a line of crested chain stitch outside the line of stem stitch, ensuring that the base of each chain rests against the stem stitch.

Work a line of evenly spaced French knots around the inside of the stem stitch, using three strands of L and keeping the knots approximately 8mm (⁵⁄₁₆") apart.

Using D, outline the inner motif with stem stitch, tapering into a single line at the point. Work a second line of stem stitch around the first, using I and beginning and ending the line before the point (*diag 2*).

Using B, work a row of crested chain stitch outside the second line of stem stitch, ensuring the base of each chain rests against the stem stitch.

Place the fabric into the hoop. Work the trellis couching over the centre of the motif, beginning with long straight stitches using I. Space the stitches approximately 1cm (³⁄₈") apart, and work a second row at right angles to the first. Couch each intersection in place with two crossed straight stitches, using two strands each of N and O blended in the needle (*diag 3*).

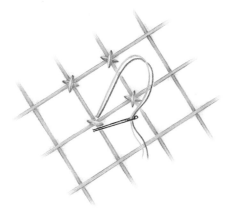

diag 3

Remove the fabric from the hoop. Work a detached chain in the centre of each square of the trellis using three strands of L.

diag 2

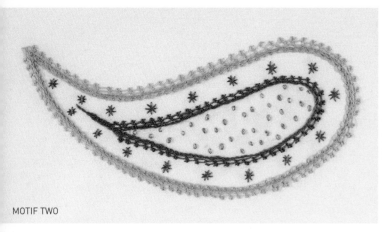

MOTIF TWO

MOTIF TWO

Two of the larger paisleys at the corners are embroidered in this manner. Using E, work a line of twisted chain stitch around the inside of the stem stitch outline. Using the same thread, work a line of crested chain stitch around the outside of the outline, ensuring the base of each chain rests against the line of stem stitch.

Using A, outline the inner motif with stem stitch, tapering into a single line at the point. Beginning and ending with stem stitches that taper into the point, work a line of crested chain stitch around the outside of the stem stitch, ensuring the base of each chain rests against the stem stitch.

Working with two strands each of N and O blended in the needle, scatter small granitos over the centre of the motif, using 3–4 stitches for each. Beginning at the point, measure and mark the placement of the terracotta stars at 2.5cm (1") intervals with the fabric marker. Using three strands of L, work four crossed straight stitches to form each star.

MOTIF THREE

The large paisley at the centre is embroidered in this manner.

Using H, embroider a line of crested chain stitch outside the line of stem stitch, ensuring that the base of each chain rests against the stem stitch. Work two lines of stem stitch around the inside of the outline using A. Add a line of evenly spaced French knots around the inside of the stem stitch, using three strands of L and keeping the knots approximately 6mm (1/4") apart.

Using F, outline the inner motif with stem stitch, tapering into a single line at the point. Changing to B, work a line of crested chain stitch around the outside of the stem stitch, ensuring that the base of each chain rests against the stem stitch.

Stitch a line of stem stitch around the inside of the motif using A, and fill the inner motif in seed stitch with B.

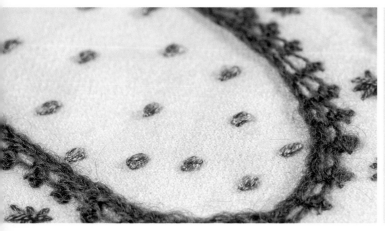

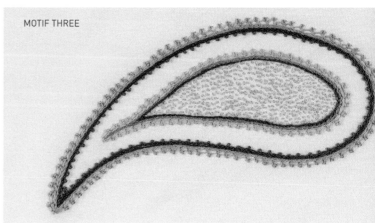

MOTIF THREE

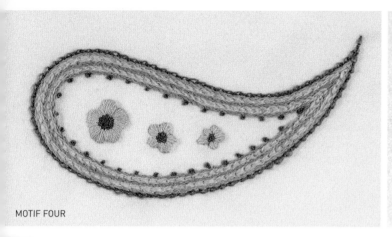

MOTIF FOUR

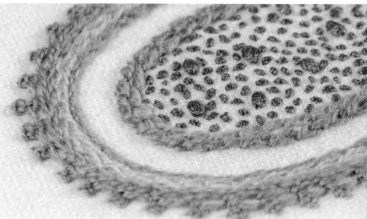

MEDIUM PAISLEY MOTIFS

Outline each medium motif in stem stitch with I.

MOTIF FOUR

Four medium motifs are worked in this manner.

Using D, work a line of twisted chain stitch around the outside of the stem stitch, tapering into a single line at the point. Embroider a line of chain stitch with J inside the stem stitch outline, then a line of stem stitch with F. Repeat these two lines, then work a line of evenly spaced French knots around the inside with D. Space the knots approximately 8mm (5/16") apart.

Change to G and outline the three flower motifs with split stitch. Covering the outline, fill the petals with satin stitch radiating out from the centre. Stitch the

centres of the flowers with closely packed French knots using three strands of L.

MOTIF FIVE

The remaining two medium paisley motifs are worked in this manner.

Embroider a line of chain stitch around the inside of the outline with J. Work a line of stem stitch inside the chain stitch using F, and a line of crested chain stitch around the outside of the outline, ensuring that the base of each chain rests against the stem stitch.

Outline the inner motif with twisted chain stitch using F. Work a second line of twisted chain stitch inside the first with C. Using three strands of L, fill the centre of the inner motif with a combination of seed stitch and granitos, using 3–4 stitches for each.

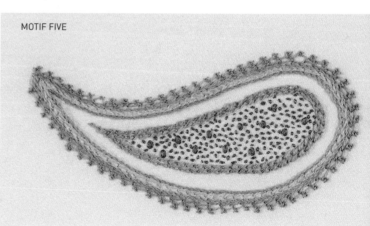

MOTIF FIVE

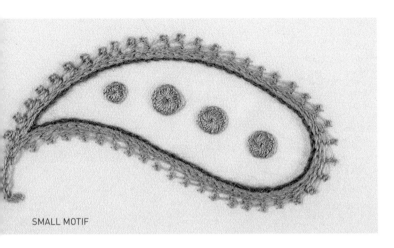

SMALL MOTIF

SMALL PAISLEY MOTIFS

The seven small paisley motifs are all worked in the same manner.

Outline each motif in stem stitch using K. Work a line of crested chain stitch outside the stem stitch outline, tapering into stem stitch at the point. Work 3–4 satin stitches at the end of the point to form the small curl.

Changing to C, work a line of stem stitch inside the outline, followed by a second line of stem stitch with D. Stitch the blanket stitch pinwheels down the centre of the shape using two strands of M.

Construction

See pages 78–84.

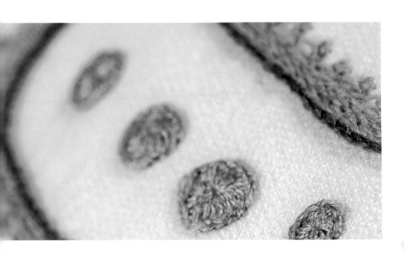

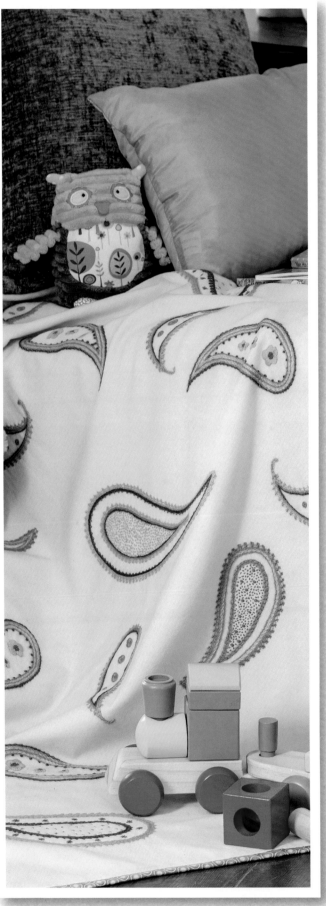

Blossoms

by Carolyn Pearce

Create a tranquil nursery with this delicate wool-embroidered blanket, scattered with posies of soft apple blossoms. This elegant design would also make a perfect gift for a mother or grandmother.

The finished blanket measures 118cm x 78cm wide (46 1/2" x 30 3/4").

This Design Uses

Colonial knot

Couching

Detached chain

Fly stitch

Grab stitch

Granitos

Raised cross stitch flower

Side ribbon stitch

Smocker's knot

Spider's web rose

Split back stitch

Straight stitch

Twisted detached chain

Whipping

Requirements

Fabric

118cm x 78cm wide (46 1/2" x 30 3/4") piece of ivory wool–cashmere blanketing

125cm x 85cm wide (49" x 33 1/2") piece of ivory print cotton

50cm x 112cm wide (20" x 44") piece of soft green print cotton

Supplies

30cm x 60cm wide (12" x 24") piece of water-soluble stabiliser

15cm (6") embroidery hoop, inner ring bound

Cream sewing thread

Pale green sewing thread

Light coloured sewing thread

Tissue paper

Fine black pen

Fine water-soluble fabric marker

Threads

Appletons crewel wool

A = 693 lt honeysuckle yellow

B = 695 med honeysuckle yellow

C = 841 lt heraldic gold

D = 851 custard yellow

E = 882 ecru (2)

Colourstreams Silken Strands

F = 51 blushing fig

DMC stranded cotton

G = 676 lt old gold

H = 922 lt copper

I = 3051 dk green-grey

J = 3052 med green-grey

Gloriana Lorikeet stranded wool

K = 120B med lt green gables

L = 120WI lt green gables

Gumnut Yarns 'Daisies' fine wool

M = 645 med khaki

Gumnut Yarns 'Poppies' silk and wool

N = 702 vy lt lemon crush

Gumnut Yarns 'Stars' stranded silk

O = 322 vy lt Pacific Ocean

Gütermann Sulky rayon 40

P = 1508 putty

Madeira Decora stranded rayon

Q = 1571 old gold

Madeira stranded silk

R = 1510 olive green

YLI silk floss

S = 114 lt olive

Ribbons

Colourstreams 4mm silk ribbon

T = 6m (6yd 21") 18 antique ivory

U = 4m (4yd 14") 43 pistache

Needles

No. 18 chenille – ribbon embroidery

No. 22 chenille – crewel wool

No. 5 crewel – all other wool;
raised cross stitch flower centres

No. 8 crewel – forget-me-nots

No. 10 crewel – all other embroidery

Preparation for Embroidery

See the liftout pattern for the embroidery design and design placement guide.

We recommend that you read the complete article and instructions on pages 78–84 relating to this project before you begin.

Transferring the design

The apple blossom posy is repeated on the blanket eight times, adjusting orientation as well as the number and placement of smaller flowers to achieve a varied appearance. Use the design placement diagram as a guide for placing the posies.

Cut eight 15cm (6") squares from the tissue paper. Trace the embroidery design onto each square of tissue paper with the black pen.

Place one of the traced designs on the blanketing at the position for the first posy and pin in place. Tack along the design lines with light coloured sewing thread. Tack the remaining embroidery designs, rotating or flipping the placement to achieve the desired effect. Score the tissue paper with the eye end of a needle and carefully tear away.

Embroidery

Refer to the close-up photograph for colour placement.

All embroidery is worked with two strands of thread unless otherwise specified.

All the posies are worked in a similar manner. Each posy has three blossoms, three open buds, three closed buds and seven leaves as indicated on the embroidery design. By varying the number and placement of the smaller flowers and ribbon leaves, each posy has its own unique look.

APPLE BLOSSOMS

Embroider each petal with an eight-stitch granitos using E. Change to one strand of K and add a straight stitch between each petal. Work a fly stitch around the tip of each petal using L for definition, and add two or three straight stitch highlights along the tip (*diag 1*).

diag 1

Work three colonial knots at the centre of the blossom using one strand of B and two strands of I blended in the needle. Change to one strand of A and two strands of H blended in the needle, and work another three colonial knots between and on top of the first.

Complete the blossom by adding three straight stitch highlights to the base of each petal using S. Work each stitch from the middle of the petal towards the base.

OPEN BUDS

Embroider the centre of the bud with an eight-stitch granitos using D. Embroider the two outer petals, each with three straight stitches, using C for the right hand petal and E for the left hand petal.

Changing to one strand of K, work four or five straight stitches over the base of the bud for the sepals, and add another straight stitch along each side of the bud for definition. Work a small six-stitch granitos for the calyx. Embroider a long straight stitch for the stem and couch in place with the same thread. Using one strand of F, whip the couched stem.

Embroider additional straight stitch highlights over the calyx and the base of the bud using one strand of F. Work two tiny fly stitches with long anchoring stitches at the tip of the bud (diag 2).

diag 2

CLOSED BUDS

Using E, embroider the bud with five close straight stitches, making the centre stitch slightly longer. Embroider the highlights, sepals, calyxes and tips in the same manner as the open buds.

STEMS

Each posy has a group of six stems. Embroider each stem in split back stitch, alternating between one strand of F and K.

LEAVES

The leaves are worked in groups of two or three. Work each leaf in close fly stitch, using two strands of K or L, or one strand of M. Start each leaf with an uneven fly stitch – short on one side and long on the other – to give it a curved tip. Add a smocker's knot at the base of each leaf using the same thread.

The remaining roses and rosebuds, ribbon leaves and forget-me-nots can be placed as you wish around each posy to acheive the desired effect.

CREAM ROSES

Work the small cream roses with raised cross stitch flowers using one strand of N. Embroider a colonial knot at the centre of each flower using one strand of J and two strands of Q blended in the needle.

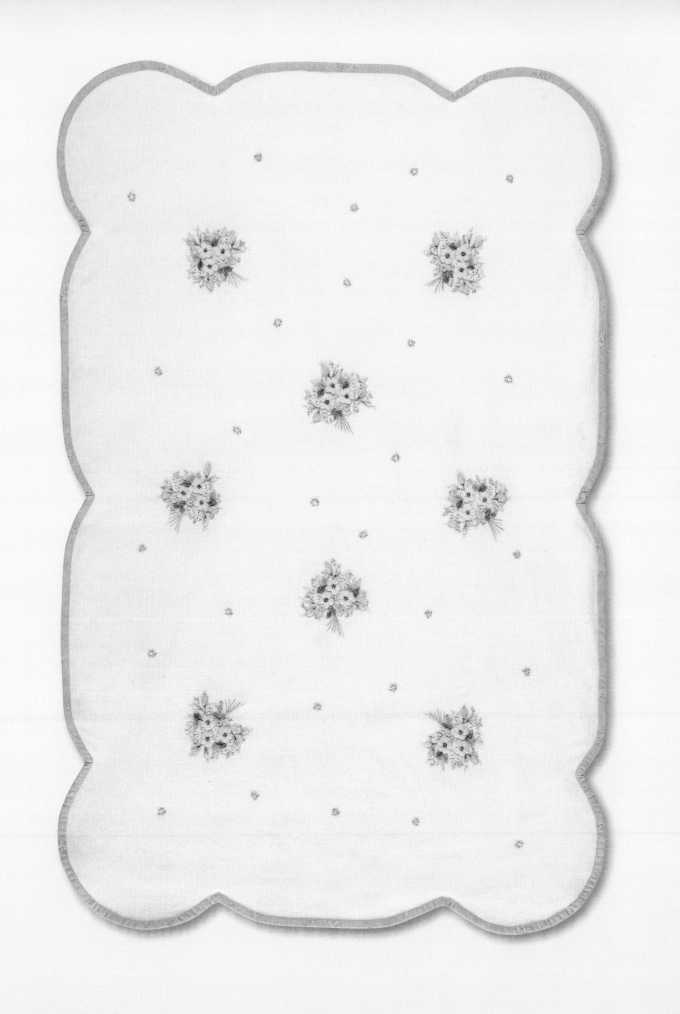

RIBBON ROSES AND ROSEBUDS

The ribbon roses are embroidered with spider's web roses. Work five straight stitch spokes for each flower using the cream sewing thread, then weave the petals with T *(diag 3)*.

diag 3

The rosebuds are composed of two side ribbon stitches worked with T, the second slightly longer than the first. For the left hand petal, insert the needle to the right hand side of the ribbon, and for the right hand petal insert the needle to the left. This helps the petals to curl inwards *(diag 4)*.

diag 4

Changing to one strand of P, embroider a large fly stitch around the base of the bud. Add two straight stitches at the tip, and a straight stitch over one of the petals *(diag 5)*.

diag 5

RIBBON LEAVES

Embroider pairs of ribbon leaves with twisted detached chains using U. Change to one strand of P and add a long straight stitch over each anchoring stitch *(diag 6)*.

diag 6

Work a fly stitch around the base of each leaf and embroider a smocker's knot over the top. Add a short straight stitch stem if necessary.

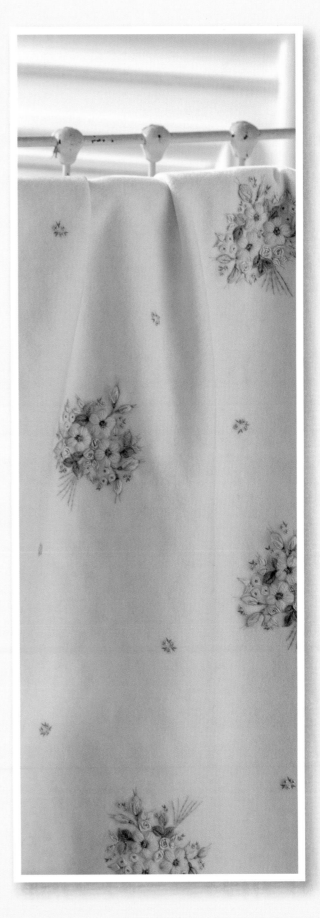

FORGET-ME-NOTS

Pairs of forget-me-nots with one set of leaves
are embroidered among the posies. Little circlets
consisting of three flowers and three sets of leaves
are scattered across the blanket.

Work the centre colonial knot first, using two strands
of G and one strand of J blended in the needle. Then
work five colonial knots for the petals, using three
strands of O. To achieve even spacing of the petals,
place the first knot directly below the centre and the
following two side by side above the centre (*diag 7*).

diag 7

To complete the flower, place a knot in the remaining
space on each side of the centre for petals four and five.

Embroider each set of leaves with one strand of
R, working two tiny detached chains with long
anchoring stitches.

Construction

See pages 78–84.

Blossoms
Shoulder Cloth
by Carolyn Pearce

The finished cloth measures
60cm x 20cm wide (23 ¹/₂" x 8").

Requirements

Supplies
White bath towel
25cm x 20mm wide (10" x ³/₄") piece of white lace
White sewing thread
4ply white crochet cotton
1.75mm (US6) crochet hook
2mm (US4) crochet hook
Tracing paper
Fine black pen

Threads
Colourstreams Silken Strands
A = 51 blushing fig
DMC stranded cotton
B = 676 lt old gold
C = 3051 dk green-grey
D = 3052 med green-grey
Gloriana Lorikeet stranded wool
E = 120B med lt green gables
F = 120WI lt green gables
Gumnut Yarns 'Poppies' silk and wool
G = 702 vy lt lemon crush
Gumnut Yarns 'Stars' stranded silk
H = 322 vy lt Pacific Ocean
Madeira Decora stranded rayon
I = 1571 old gold
Madeira stranded silk
J = 1510 olive green

Needles
No. 5 crewel
No. 8 crewel
No. 10 crewel

Preparation for Embroidery

See the liftout pattern for the cloth template.

Preparing the fabric

Trace the cloth template onto the tracing paper with the black pen and cut out. Avoiding the hems and ensuring a section of the woven band is positioned 7.5cm (3") from one short end of the piece, pin the template onto one corner of the towel *(diag 1)*.

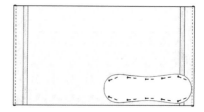

diag 1

Cut out. You should be able to get six cloths from a standard towel. Neaten the raw edges with an overlock or machine zigzag stitch.

Embroidery

Refer to the template in the liftout pattern for stitch placement.

The no. 5 crewel needle is used with the wool and for the raised cross stitch flower centres. The no. 8 needle is used for the forget-me-nots, and the no. 10 needle for all other embroidery.

All embroidery is worked with one strand of thread unless otherwise specified.

Measure and mark the centre of the woven band. Embroider three cream roses around the centre point in the same manner as the blanket, using G for the flower, and two strands of I and one strand of C blended in the needle for the centre.

This Design Uses

Colonial knot

Detached chain

Fly stitch

Raised cross stitch flower

Smocker's knot

Split back stitch

Straight stitch

To the right of the cream roses, embroider two buds. Work four straight stitches with two strands of G for each bud. Add a calyx, sepals and highlights using A and E, in the same manner as the blanket. Add a straight stitch in E for each stem.

Using E, work a pair of fly stitch leaves to the left of the roses. Add a smocker's knot at the base of each leaf. Change to F and embroider a third leaf above the roses in the same manner.

Work the two pairs of forget-me-nots in the same manner as the blanket. Use two strands of B and one strand of D blended in the needle for the centre, and three strands of H for the petals. Changing to J, add a pair of tiny detached chain leaves to each set of forget-me-nots, in the same manner as the blanket.

Finally, work the three stems in split back stitch using E.

Construction

Lightly press the embroidery from the wrong side. Tack the lace in position over the back of the embroidered band, turning the raw ends under. Handstitch in place with the white sewing thread, ensuring the stitches are not visible on the right side of the cloth.

Complete the shoulder cloth by working a crochet border around the edge with the crochet cotton.

I would like to thank Lucy Lazzaro for her beautiful work crocheting the border – **Carolyn**

CROCHET BORDER

First row: Use the 1.75mm (US6) crochet hook. Work a row of single crochet, with the stitches approximately 7mm (5/16") apart, around the edge of the cloth. The total number of stitches should be divisible by three. Slipstitch into the first single crochet (*diag 1*).

Second row: Use the 2mm (US4) crochet hook. Work four chains. Work four trebles into the same single crochet as the slipstitch finishing the first round. Miss two single crochet, slipstitch into the next single crochet.

Work four chain, four trebles into the same single crochet as the slipstitch, miss two single crochet, slipstitch into the next single crochet (*diag 2*). Repeat from * to * around the edge to the start of the round. Slipstitch into the first chain of the second round.

diag 1   *diag 2*

Cut the yarn, leaving a long tail. Using the hook, catch the tail and pull it through the last loop. Tighten the tail to secure the last stitch. Weave in the ends.

Wee Willie Winkie

by Annette Drysdale

When it's time for all good children to be in bed, this charming cuddle blanket is perfect for snuggling under. The endearing thread painted Wee Willie Winkie is sure to be your child's best friend in the land of nod!

The finished blanket measures 115cm x 75cm wide (45 $\frac{1}{4}$" x 29 $\frac{1}{2}$").

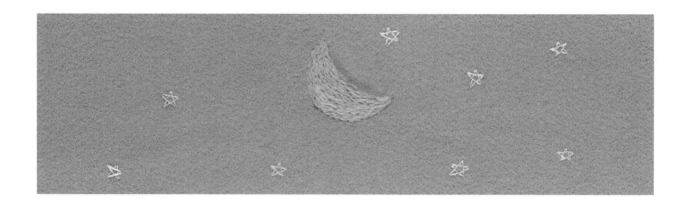

Requirements

Fabric

115cm x 75cm wide (45 ¼" x 29 ½") piece of pale blue wool/cashmere velour blanketing

128cm x 88cm wide (50 ⅜" x 34 ⅝") piece of multi-coloured print cotton

Supplies

3.6m (4yd) red mini piping

40cm x 50cm wide (16" x 20") piece of water-soluble stabiliser

Tracing paper

30cm (12") embroidery hoop

Black pony beads (3)

Matching sewing thread

Fine water-soluble fabric marker

Fine brown permanent pen

Threads

Appletons crewel wool
A = 202 vy lt flame red
B = 464 dk cornflower
C = 503 med scarlet
D = 553 lt bright yellow
E = 703 lt flesh tint
F = 876 lt pastel blue
G = 991B bright white

Au Ver à Soie, Fine d'Aubusson
H = 1770 brown black
I = 3742 café au lait

DMC no. 5 perlé cotton
J = 321 vy lt garnet
K = 729 med old gold
L = 782 dk topaz
M = 796 dk royal blue

DMC stranded cotton
N = 310 black
O = B5200 snow white

DMC stranded rayon
P = 30666 bright Christmas red
Q = 35200 snow white

Gumnut Yarns 'Daisies' fine wool
R = 947 dk hazelnut

Gumnut Yarns 'Stars' stranded silk
S = 708 dk lemon crush
T = 992 lt pewter

Needles

No. 22 chenille
No. 8 crewel
No. 9 milliner's

Preparation for Embroidery

See the liftout pattern for the embroidery design.

We recommend that you read the complete article and instructions on pages 78–84 relating to this project before you begin.

Preparing the fabric

Fold the blanketing in half lengthwise and tack along the foldline. Unfold. Measure 50cm (19 ¾") from the bottom edge along the tacked line and fold at this point. Tack along the foldline and unfold.

Transferring the design

Using the brown permanent pen, trace the embroidery design and placement marks onto the water-soluble stabiliser. Aligning the placement marks with the tacked lines, pin the water-soluble stabiliser onto the blanketing. Tack around the edge of the stabiliser, then 6mm (¼") away from the design outlines.

Embroidery

See the liftout pattern for the stitch direction diagram.

Refer to the close-up photograph for colour placement.

Use the no. 9 milliner's needle for the bullion loops, the no. 22 chenille needle with the crewel wool and the no. 8 crewel needle for all other embroidery.

All embroidery is worked in the hoop with one strand of thread unless otherwise specified.

FACE, NIGHTCAP AND HAIR

Outline the eye with back stitch using N, and fill with a few small straight stitches using O. Change back to N and add a seed stitch for the pupil.

Embroider the outline of the ear in stem stitch with A. Fill the ear with split stitch using E, then change back to A and work a seed stitch for the centre of the ear (*diag 1*).

diag 1

Stitching from the forehead to the chin, fill the face with long and short stitch using E. Embroider the neck with long and short stitch, using E at the centre and A at the outer edges. Change to R and embroider the eyebrow with back stitch. Add short straight stitch eyelashes using N. Outline the face in back stitch with I, and add a small curved row of back stitch for the cheek.

Stitching from the base to the tip, embroider the nightcap with long and short stitch using B. Change to J and add straight stitch stars over the top, working four straight stitches for each. Fill the pompom with Ghiordes knots. Cut, trim and brush up the tufts to form a soft dome.

Using R, embroider the hair with closely packed 10–16 wrap bullion loops, varying the direction of each loop.

NIGHTGOWN, ARMS AND LEGS

Working from the lower edges towards the neck, fill the nightgown with long and short stitch, using G for the main sections and F for the shaded sections where the inside of the gown shows *(diag 2)*.

diag 2

Embroider the sleeves in a similar manner, stitching from the shoulder towards the wrist and changing the direction of the stitches around the elbows. Change to F and add the shading on the nightgown over the top of the white stitching. Embroider the cuffs in long and short stitch with C. Add three colonial knots for the buttons. Work the outlines in back stitch using H, after the legs are embroidered.

Beginning each at the top of the limb, embroider the legs with long and short stitch using E. Add the shading at the outer edges with A over the previous stitching.

Working each from the toe, fill the slippers with long and short stitch using C. Change to H and add back stitch outlines. Work closely packed Ghiordes knots for the pompoms on top of each slipper with M. Cut, trim and brush up the tufts to form a soft dome.

Embroider the hands with straight stitch using E, adding shading along each side with A. Add a few stitches over the fingers and thumb with the same thread after the clock is embroidered. Outline the arms, legs and hands with back stitch using I.

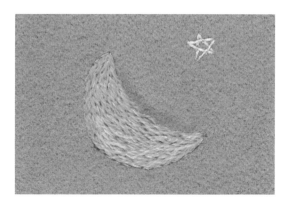

TEDDY BEAR AND CLOCK

Fill the teddy bear, including the feet, with closely packed Ghiordes knots, alternating between K and L. Cut and trim the knots, shaping the tufts to form divisions between the neck, head and ears. Dome the shapes gently at the outer edges.

Stitch the black beads in place for the eyes and nose. Embroider a fly stitch for the mouth using two strands of N, pulling the stitch into the pile *(diag 3)*.

(diag 3)

Embroider the clock face with satin stitch using two strands of Q. Change to two strands of N and add straight stitches for the hands, and seed stitches for the numbers. Using two strands of P, add three rows of stem stitch above and below the clock face. Embroider the legs with straight stitch and the bells with satin stitch.

COBBLESTONES AND SKY

Embroider the cobblestones with whipped chain stitch using R, keeping the chain stitches short.

Fill the moon with long and short stitch using D. Changing to S, add straight stitch highlights and work the outline in back stitch.

Embroider the stars around the moon using two strands of T. Work five straight stitches to form a star, each stitch interlocking the previous.

Add a tiny couching stitch over each junction to complete the couched star *(diag 4)*.

diag 4

Construction

See pages 78–84.

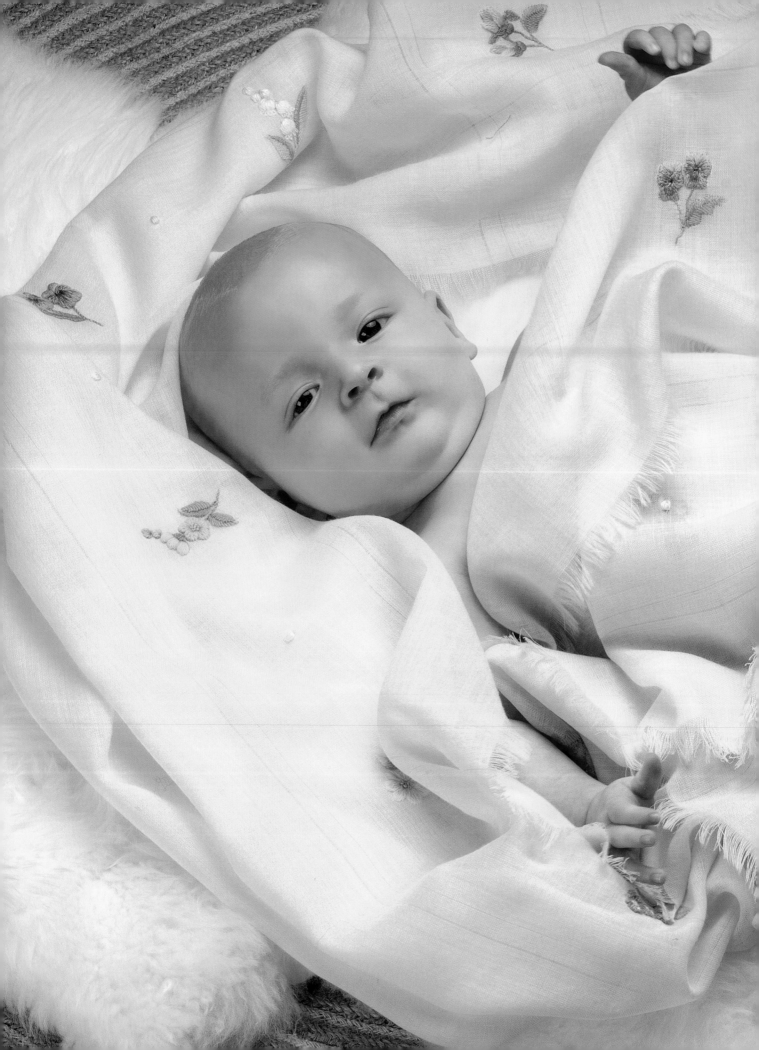

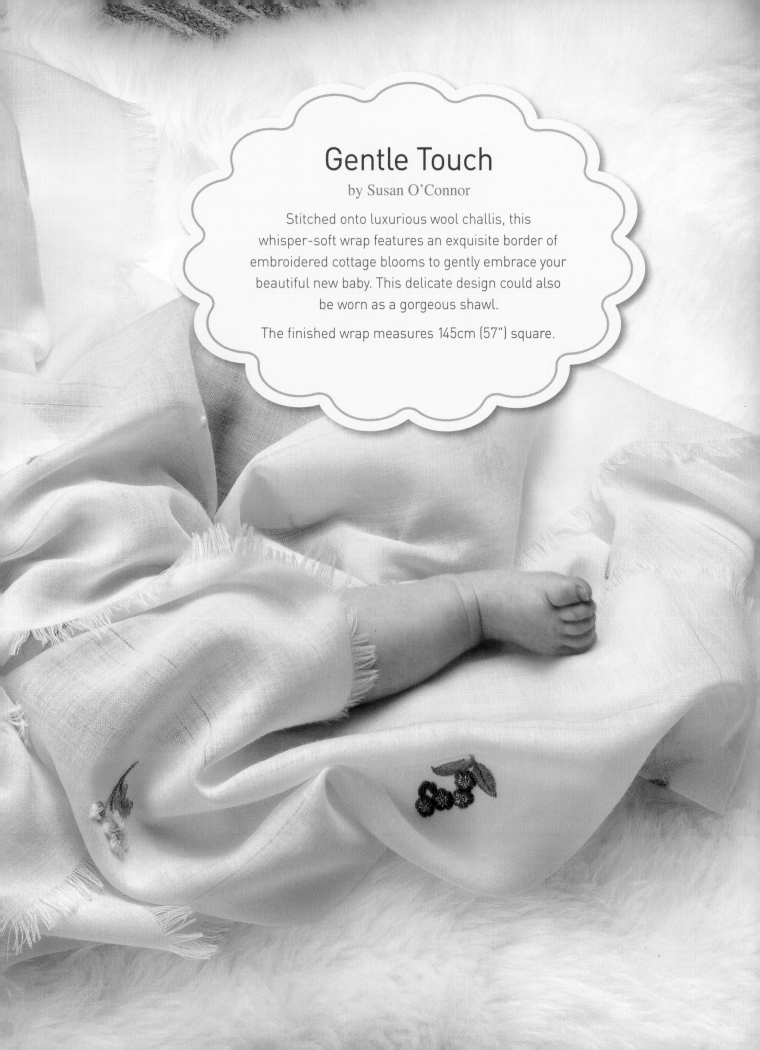

Gentle Touch
by Susan O'Connor

Stitched onto luxurious wool challis, this whisper-soft wrap features an exquisite border of embroidered cottage blooms to gently embrace your beautiful new baby. This delicate design could also be worn as a gorgeous shawl.

The finished wrap measures 145cm (57") square.

This Design Uses

Blanket stitch

Detached chain

Fly stitch

French knot

Granitos

Padded satin stitch

Satin stitch

Split stitch

Stem stitch

Straight stitch

Requirements

Fabric

145cm x 150cm wide (57" x 59") cream wool challis

Supplies

10cm (4") embroidery hoop

Tracing paper

Fine black pen

Fine water-soluble fabric marker

Threads
Au Ver à Soie, Fine d'Aubusson

A = 1012 shell pink

B = 1421 lt petrol blue

C = 2131 ultra lt yellow-green

D = 2132 lt yellow-green

E = 2542 lt yellow-orange

F = 3042 dk mushroom

G = 3484 lt mushroom

H = 4098 ivory

I = 4147 lt shell pink

Au Ver à Soie, Soie d'Alger

J = crème

K = 1013 med shell pink

L = 2131 ultra lt yellow-green

M = 2542 lt yellow-orange

N = 3432 dk mushroom

Needles

No. 24 chenille

No. 10 crewel

Preparation for Embroidery

See the liftout pattern for the embroidery designs.

We recommend that you read the complete article before you begin.

Preparing the fabric

The fabric for this project must be cut along the grainlines to ensure perfectly straight edges. To do so, gently pull a fabric thread close to one cut edge and carefully cut along the pulled thread line. Repeat along the opposite cut edge. Pull a thread and trim along each side, just back from the selvedge, to create a piece 145cm (57") square.

Working on one edge at a time, remove the crosswise threads for a depth of 1.5cm (⅝") to form a fringe around the wrap (*diag 1*).

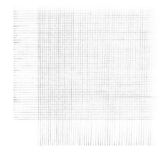

diag 1

Drawn thread border

All measurements are taken from the solid edge of the fabric, not the edge of the fringing.

Measure 9cm (3½") from one edge and carefully remove one thread across the width of the fabric. Remove a second thread in the same manner. Measure 1cm (⅜") from these removed threads and remove one thread across the width of the fabric (*diag 2*).

diag 2

Measure 10cm (4") from the innermost removed thread, and remove one thread in the same manner.

Measure another 1cm (³⁄₈") and remove two threads as before. Repeat for the three remaining sides *(diag 3)*.

All embroidery is worked within the border formed by the pulled thread lines.

diag 3

Transferring the design

Wool fabrics have a naturally high moisture content and, as this design is transferred with a water-soluble fabric marker, each design is best transferred just before working the embroidery.

Trace each design onto a separate piece of tracing paper with the black pen.

CORNER SPRAY

Each corner is embroidered with a rosebud spray. Slide the design under the fabric, centring the rosebud diagonally in the corner square that results from withdrawing the threads *(diag 4)*.

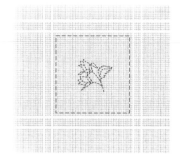

diag 4

Pin the fabric to the paper and carefully transfer the design with the fabric marker. Repeat for the remaining three corners.

SIDE SPRAYS

The placement of the designs is the same for each side.

Fold the wrap in half across the width and mark the foldline at the centre of the border with a pin. This is the position for the pink anemone spray. Centre the design under the fabric and transfer using the fabric marker.

Space the remaining four motifs 18cm (7") apart between the corner and centre sprays. Centre each design vertically between the borders and transfer using the fabric marker. Repeat along the remaining three sides, placing the flower sprays in the same sequence along each side.

GRANITOS

After completing all the flower sprays along each edge, measure and mark the centre point between each spray for the granitos.

Embroidery

Refer to the close-up photographs for colour placement.

Use the chenille needle for the wool and the crewel needle for the silk.

All embroidery is worked in the hoop with one strand unless otherwise specified.

Take extra care when tightening the fabric in the hoop, as the weave is very easily distorted. After completing each motif, remove the hoop carefully. If the fabric weave has been disrupted, gently stroke across the distorted area with the eye end of a needle until the fabric threads resume their original position.

ROSEBUD

Using I, outline the outer petals with split stitch. Fill each petal with three layers of satin stitch padding, working the first layer across the shape. Work satin stitch over the padding, stitching over the split stitch edge and angling the stitches towards the base of the petal. Changing to A, outline the centre petal with split stitch. Pad and cover with satin stitch in the same manner as the outer petals. Work several straight stitches over the lower part of the outer petals for the shading, angling the stitches towards the base of the petals.

Using K, work three straight stitches over the tip of the centre petal *(diag 5)*.

diag 5

Outline the receptacle and sepals in split stitch with D. Continue working lines of split stitch around the inside of the sepals until they are full. Work three layers of satin stitch padding in the receptacle, beginning with a horizontal layer. Cover with satin stitch, working over the split stitch outline. Using the same thread, stitch the stems in stem stitch and the leaf in fly stitch.

PINK ANEMONE

Outline the petals of the open and partially open flowers in split stitch with I. Pad each petal with two layers of satin stitch padding, placing the first layer of stitches down length of the petal. Cover each petal with satin stitch, working over the split stitch outline. Stitch the lower bud with two layers of satin stitch, angling the stitches into the base of the bud. Changing to A, work a straight stitch between each flower petal to define the shapes. Work three straight stitches over the base of each petal on the open flower and over the base of the bud for the veins. Using the same thread, stitch the small bud at the tip with two layers of satin stitch, angling the stitches towards the base.

Work French knots in the centre of the open flower, blending one strand each of E and M in the needle.

Using D, outline the calyx of the partially open flower with split stitch. Pad the calyx with two layers of satin stitch padding, beginning with a vertical layer. Cover the calyx with satin stitch, working over the split stitch outline.

Using the same thread, work the stems in stem stitch and the leaves in fly stitch. Work a fly stitch at the base of each bud for the calyx, adding a small straight stitch over the centre of the base of the upper bud *(diag 6)*.

diag 6

ROSEBUD

PINK ANEMONE

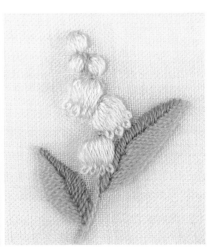

LILY-OF-THE-VALLEY

DAISY

HEARTSEASE

FORGET-ME-NOT

LILY-OF-THE-VALLEY

Outline the three large flowers with split stitch using H. Pad each flower with three layers of satin stitch padding, placing the first layer across each shape. Work satin stitch over the padding, stitching over the split stitch edge and angling the stitches towards the top of the flower.

Stitch the small buds with two layers of satin stitch using H, angling the stitches towards the top. Work straight stitch highlights at the top of the flowers and buds using J.

Changing to D, stitch the stem in stem stitch and add a fly stitch calyx at the top of each flower and bud. Work the leaves in satin stitch, using D on the narrow side and C on the wider side.

Embroider four detached chains along the lower edge of each flower with H.

DAISY

Using H, outline each petal with split stitch and cover with satin stitch, angling the stitches towards the centre of the flower. Change to E and add a straight stitch between each petal to define the shapes. Using L, work three straight stitches over the base of each petal for the veins. Changing back to E, fill the centre of the flower with two-wrap French knots.

Outline the upper edges of the bud in split stitch using H. Fill the petals with two layers of satin stitch padding, starting with a horizontal layer. Cover with satin stitch enclosing the outline. Outline the calyx of the bud with split stitch using C. Fill the calyx with padded satin stitch in the same manner as the bud. Using D, work 5–6 straight stitches over the base of the calyx, angling the stitches towards the stem.

Embroider the stem and leaf vein in stem stitch using D. Fill the leaf with detached chains, working each from the centre vein to the edge of the leaf.

HEARTSEASE

Using G, outline the three lower petals with split stitch. Fill the petals with satin stitch padding, working three layers of padding for the lower petal and two for each of the side petals. Ensure that the last layer of padding is worked at right angles to the covering satin stitch. Cover the petals with satin stitch, angling the stitches towards the centre of the flower and placing the stitches over the outlines.

Outline the two upper petals with split stitch using E. Cover the petals with satin stitch, angling the stitches towards the centre of the flower in a similar manner to the lower petals. Work 3–5 straight stitches over the base of each of the three lower petals with F for the veins. Repeat with N for the highlights. Stitch a French knot at the centre of each flower using two strands of D.

Using one strand of D, embroider the stems in stem stitch. Partially work a detached chain at the base of the leaf, without anchoring the stitch. Continue around the leaf in blanket stitch (*diag 7*).

diag 7

Gradually change the direction of the stitches around the tip of the leaf and continue down the opposite side.

FORGET-ME-NOT

Using B, outline the flower petals with split stitch then cover with satin stitch, enclosing the outline and angling the stitches towards the centre of the flower. Embroider the buds using the same thread, working two layers of satin stitch and angling the stitches towards the tips. Work three straight stitches over the base of each petal on the open flowers with J. Using two strands of E, add a French knot at the centre of each flower.

Work a fly stitch calyx at the top of each bud with D, and embroider the stem in stem stitch. Work the leaves in blanket stitch, beginning each one with a detached chain in the same manner as the heartsease.

SPOTS

Using H, embroider a granitos at each marked point, working 6–7 stitches for each.

Finishing

Using a damp cloth, remove all visible design lines. Place the embroidery face down on a well-padded surface and press carefully.

Puppy Fun
by Louise Spriggs

What child wouldn't love to have these adorable
puppies to cuddle? Created with cosy wool
felt and simple stitches, even a new stitcher
will have these naughty little puppies romping
across this enchanting blanket in no time.

The finished blanket measures
110cm x 80cm wide (43 ½" x 31 ½").

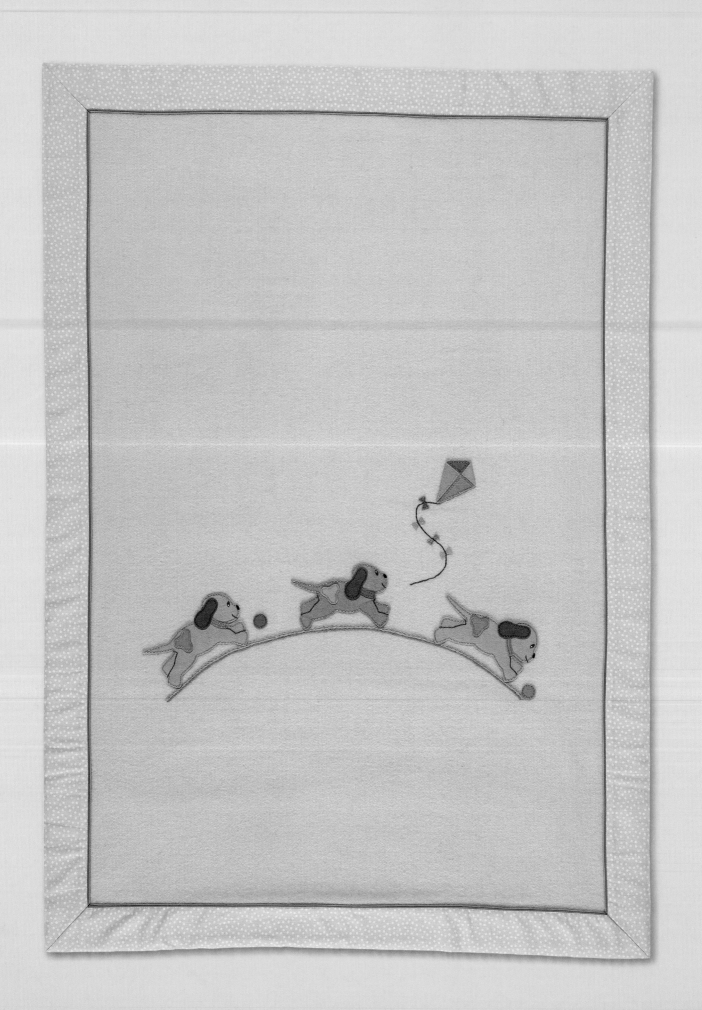

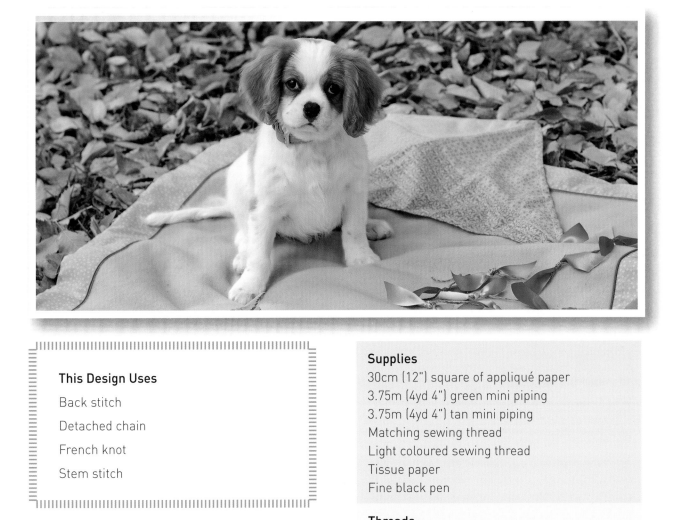

This Design Uses

Back stitch

Detached chain

French knot

Stem stitch

Supplies

30cm (12") square of appliqué paper

3.75m (4yd 4") green mini piping

3.75m (4yd 4") tan mini piping

Matching sewing thread

Light coloured sewing thread

Tissue paper

Fine black pen

Threads
Appletons crewel wool

A = 241 vy lt olive green

B = 343 lt mid olive green

C = 542 vy lt early English green

DMC stranded cotton

D = 310 black

E = 741 med tangerine

F = 799 med Delft

G = 839 chocolate

H = 841 lt beige

I = 3045 dk yellow-beige

J = 3341 apricot

K = 3810 med teal

L = 3865 winter white

Needles

No. 22 chenille

No. 4 crewel

No. 8 crewel

Requirements

Fabric

110cm x 80cm wide (43 ½" x 31 ½") piece of sage green wool blanketing

125cm x 95cm wide (50" x 38") piece of tan and white polka dot print cotton

10cm x 30cm wide (4" x 12") piece of caramel wool felt

12cm x 15cm wide (5" x 6") piece of grey-brown wool felt

5cm x 10cm wide (2" x 4") piece of chocolate brown wool felt

3cm x 6cm wide (2" x 3") piece of peach felt

3cm (2") square of orange felt

5cm x 18cm wide (2" x 7") piece of periwinkle felt

3cm x 10cm wide (2" x 4") piece of teal felt

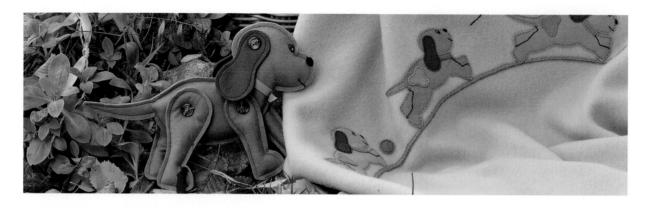

Preparation for Embroidery

See the liftout pattern for the embroidery design and felt templates.

We recommend that you read the complete article and instructions on pages 78–84 relating to this project before you begin.

Transferring the design

Fold the blanketing in half widthwise and tack along the foldline. Unfold and repeat in the opposite direction to mark the centre.

Trace the embroidery design and placement marks onto the tissue paper with the black pen. Position the tracing over the blanketing, aligning the placement marks with the tacked lines, and pin in place. Tack along the design lines with the light coloured sewing thread. Using the eye end of a needle, score the tissue paper along the tacked lines then tear away the paper.

Preparing the felt

PUPPIES

Trace the templates for the puppy body, patch, ear and collar three times each, and the ball twice onto the appliqué paper. Cut out roughly around each outline. Fuse two body pieces and one patch onto the caramel felt, and one body and two patches onto the grey-brown felt. Fuse the three ear pieces onto the chocolate brown felt, two collars and one ball onto the periwinkle felt, and one collar and one ball onto the teal felt.

Cut out each piece along the marked lines. Remove the backing paper from the teal collar and carefully fuse in place onto the grey-brown body piece. Repeat for the remaining two collars and body pieces.

Fuse the patches to the bodies in the same manner, placing the caramel patch on the grey-brown body, and a grey-brown patch on each of the caramel bodies. Finally, fuse an ear onto each puppy, varying the position of each slightly.

KITE

Trace the kite bow four times onto the appliqué paper and cut out roughly. Fuse one bow each to the blue, teal, peach and orange felt pieces. Cut out along the outline and remove the backing paper.

Trace the kite triangles and base onto the appliqué paper and cut out roughly. Fuse the two smaller triangles to the teal and orange felts, and the larger triangles to the peach and periwinkle felts. Cut out along the outlines and remove the backing paper. Fuse the base shape to the periwinkle felt and cut out.

Aligning the outer edges, carefully position the triangles over the base shape and fuse in place.

Embroidery

Refer to the close-up photograph for colour placement.

Use the no. 4 crewel needle with six strands of cotton and the no. 8 crewel with three strands. The chenille needle is used for the wool.

All embroidery is worked in back stitch unless otherwise specified. Use one strand when stitching with the wool and three strands for the stranded cotton. Use six strands of cotton for the kite string.

HILL

Using A, B or C, embroider the hill with three close rows of stem stitch. Use A for the top row, C for the middle row and B for the lower row.

PUPPIES

The initial embroidery on the puppies is worked before they are attached to the blanket.

Using H for the grey-brown felt and I for the caramel felt, work a line of stitching just inside the edge of each patch. Repeat for the collars, using F for the periwinkle collars and K for the teal collar. Embroider around the ears in G, leaving any sections where the ear is not attached to the body unstitched.

Embroider the definition lines for the legs on each puppy using G, and add a curved line for the mouth. You can draw these first with a water-soluble fabric marker if you are more comfortable stitching along a marked line. Change to D and work a small detached chain for the nose very close to the edge of the felt. Add another two detached chains around the first *(diag 1)*.

diag 1

Work the eye in a similar manner using G, and add a French knot with L for the highlight.

Position the puppies on the blanket, with the grey-brown dog in the middle, and pin in place. Change to I and embroider the outline of the outer two puppies. Where the existing stitching for the legs and mouth meets the edge, slide your needle under the stitch, so the new stitching sits underneath *(diag 2)*.

diag 2

Embroider the outline of the centre dog in a similar manner using H.

BALLS

Remove the backing paper from the balls. Position the periwinkle ball in front of the first dog, at the end of the hill. Hold it in place with a few tacking stitches, and fuse. Embroider the outline using F. Repeat for the teal ball in front of the third dog, using K.

KITE

Remove the backing paper from the bows. Position each bow along the tacked line for the kite string, hold in place with a few tacking stitches, and fuse. Embroider the outline of each, using K for the teal bow, J for the peach, F for the periwinkle, and E for the orange. Embroider the kite string using six strands of G, working a stitch over each bow.

Embroider the inner two outlines of each kite triangle, using E for the orange felt, K for the teal, J for the peach and F for the periwinkle *(diag 3)*.

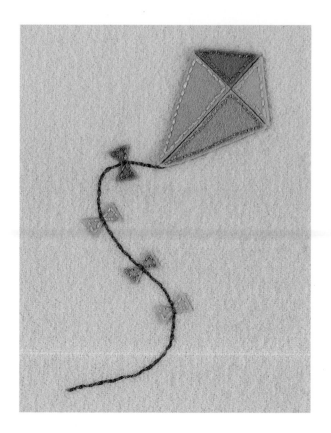

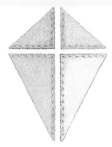

diag 3

Remove the backing paper from the base piece and pin in place on the blanket, covering the end of the kite string. Complete the outlines on the outer edges of each triangle with the corresponding colours to secure the kite *(diag 4)*.

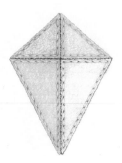

diag 4

Construction

See pages 78–84.

Puppy Fun toy

by Louise Spriggs

Either as a perfect obedient companion to the matching puppy blanket or as a special gift just on its own, you won't be able to resist giving this cute felt puppy a happy home in your child's playbox.

The finished toy measures
19cm high x 29cm long (7 ½" x 11 ½").

This Design Uses

Back stitch

Detached chain

French knot

Requirements

Fabric

20cm x 30cm wide (8" x 12") piece of grey-brown wool felt (2)

15cm x 25cm wide (6" x 10") piece of chocolate brown wool felt

Supplies

15mm (⅝") tortoiseshell buttons (6)

25cm x 10mm wide (10" x ⅜") piece of aqua grosgrain ribbon

Matching sewing thread

Fibre fill

Tracing paper

Large darning needle

Fabric sealant

Fine black pen

Fine water-soluble fabric marker

Threads
DMC stranded cotton

A = 310 black

B = 839 chocolate

C = 841 lt beige

D = 3865 winter white

Needles

No. 4 crewel needle

Preparation for Embroidery

See the liftout pattern for the ear, leg and body templates.

We recommend that you read the complete article before you begin.

Transferring the design

Using a lightbox or window, trace the body template, including markings, twice onto the tracing paper with the black pen. Repeat for the two leg templates and the ear template, tracing each four times. Use the large darning needle to pierce a hole at the marked points for the eyes, nose, mouth and buttons.

Pin the two ear pieces to the chocolate brown felt and cut out. Use the fabric marker to mark the point for the button through the pierced hole. Pin the remaining pieces of tracing paper to the grey-brown felt and cut out, transferring the marked points in the same manner.

Embroidery

Refer to the close-up photograph for colour placement.

Use the no. 4 crewel needle with six strands of cotton for all embroidery.

Embroider the mouth in back stitch on each body piece using B. Work the eyes with four detached chains around each other, in a similar manner to the blanket. Add a French knot at the centre of each eye with D.

Construction

All seams are 6mm (¼") unless otherwise specified.

Pin and stitch two ear pieces together, matching raw edges. Repeat for the remaining ear. Pin and stitch corresponding pairs of legs and the body, leaving the marked openings unstitched. Fill each piece with fibre fill before stitching the remainder of the seam.

Pin an ear to each side of the head, matching the marked points for the buttons. Thread a 10cm (4") length of C. Holding a button in position over one

ear, take the needle through the button, pierce the head, and emerge through a second button on the other side. Leave a 5cm (2") tail. Thread a second length of C through the buttons, using the holes diagonally opposite the first *(diag 1)*.

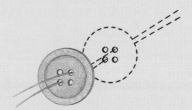

diag 1

Knot the thread tails on either side firmly three times and trim the tails neatly. Repeat with the remaining two holes of the buttons.

Attach the legs in the same manner. Secure all of the knots with a small amount of fabric sealant.

Embroider the nose through both layers of the felt with A, working detached chains on each side in a similar manner to the eye. Tie the length of grosgrain ribbon around the neck and trim the tails.

Mary's Little Lamb

by Susan O'Connor

Bring delight to a little girl's heart with this gorgeous thread painted design. The beloved nursery rhyme character, Mary, and her faithful little lamb are lovingly recreated in soft crewel wools stitched onto pastel pink blanketing as soft as a lamb. Your special little girl is sure to want to take it wherever she goes!

The finished blanket measures 110cm x 80cm wide (43 1/4" x 31 1/2").

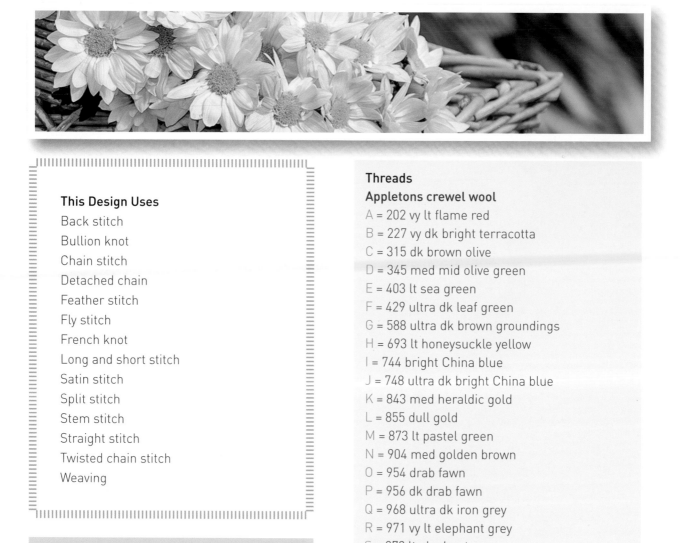

This Design Uses

Back stitch

Bullion knot

Chain stitch

Detached chain

Feather stitch

Fly stitch

French knot

Long and short stitch

Satin stitch

Split stitch

Stem stitch

Straight stitch

Twisted chain stitch

Weaving

Requirements

Fabric

110cm x 80cm wide (43 ¼" x 31 ½") piece of pink wool – cashmere velour blanketing

130cm x 100cm wide (51 ¼" x 39 ⅜") piece of blue diagonal gingham print cotton

Supplies

20cm x 30cm wide (8" x 12") piece of white wool felt (2)

White machine sewing thread

25cm (10") embroidery hoop

Tracing paper

Tissue paper

Fine black pen

Fine water-soluble marker

Threads

Appletons crewel wool

A = 202 vy lt flame red

B = 227 vy dk bright terracotta

C = 315 dk brown olive

D = 345 med mid olive green

E = 403 lt sea green

F = 429 ultra dk leaf green

G = 588 ultra dk brown groundings

H = 693 lt honeysuckle yellow

I = 744 bright China blue

J = 748 ultra dk bright China blue

K = 843 med heraldic gold

L = 855 dull gold

M = 873 lt pastel green

N = 904 med golden brown

O = 954 drab fawn

P = 956 dk drab fawn

Q = 968 ultra dk iron grey

R = 971 vy lt elephant grey

S = 972 lt elephant grey

T = 975 dk elephant grey

U = 992 off white

V = 995 cherry red

Au ver à Soie, Fine d'Aubusson

W = 1760 chocolate brown

X = 4113 dk flesh

Cascade House shaded crewel wool

Y = 1000/4 white

Z = 4160/6 rose pink

AA = 7280/4 lt olive green

Needles

No. 24 chenille

No.15 long darner

No. 24 tapestry

Preparation for Embroidery

See the liftout pattern for the embroidery design and felt templates.

We recommend that you read the complete article and instructions on pages 78–84 relating to this project before you begin.

Preparing the fabric

Fold the blanketing in half lengthwise and tack along the foldline. Unfold. Measure 42cm (16 ½") from the bottom edge along the tacked line and fold widthwise at this point. Tack along the foldline and unfold.

Transferring the design

Trace the embroidery design and placement marks along the black lines onto the tissue paper with the black pen. Position the tracing over the blanketing, aligning the placement marks with the tacked lines, and pin in place. Tack along the design lines with the white sewing thread. Score along the tacked lines with the eye end of a needle and carefully remove the tissue paper. This marks the embroidery design and the positions for the felt padding.

Using the black pen, trace the outlines and internal design lines of the felt templates for Mary and the lamb onto separate pieces of tracing paper.

Position a tracing over a lightbox or window and tape in place. Position a piece of white felt over the tracing and tape in place. Trace the design onto the felt with the black pen. Cut out the shape along the outline using sharp scissors. Repeat for the remaining tracing and felt.

Position the felt shapes over the blanket and pin in place. Using the white sewing thread, tack the felt in place and remove the pins *(diag 1)*.

(diag 1)

Embroidery

See the liftout pattern for the stitch direction diagrams.

Refer to the close-up photographs for colour placement.

Use the no. 15 long darner for the bullion knots, the no. 24 tapestry needle for the weaving and the no. 24 chenille needle for all other embroidery.

All embroidery except the lettering is worked in the hoop. Use one strand of wool unless otherwise specified and take the outermost stitches over the edge of the felt, ensuring it is completely covered by embroidery.

Hint

As an alternative to tacking, position the designs by placing Mary's right foot up 36cm (14 ½") and in 27cm (10 ⅝") from the right hand edge. Place the lamb's centre left leg up 28cm (11") and in 28cm (11") from the left hand edge. You can then write the text in freehand with a water-soluble fabric marker – Susan

Mary had... a little lamb...

MARY
CLOTHING AND BOOTS

Alternating between I and U, embroider the skirt stripes in close rows of stem stitch. The lines on the skirt correspond with the centres of the blue stripes. Stitching from the shoulder to the cuff, embroider the left hand blouse sleeve in long and short stitch using L. Work the cuff in satin stitch with the same thread. Changing to K, work the shading and fold lines over the previous stitches in straight stitch. Embroider the shoulder of the right hand sleeve above the blackboard in a similar manner.

Change to J and embroider the jacket body with long and short stitch in a similar manner to the sleeve. Work the jacket sleeve in satin stitch and define the lower edge with a line of split stitch using the same thread.

Embroider the boot uppers in long and short stitch using P. Work the soles and the boot markings in straight stitch and stem stitch using G. Add the buttons in French knots using the same thread. Work the skirt outlines in stem stitch with G.

BLACKBOARD AND APPLE

Fill the centre of the blackboard with long and short stitch using Q. Change to C and embroider rows of chain stitch for the border.

Work the hands in satin stitch and long and short stitch using A. Change to W and define the hand outlines in back stitch.

Fill the apple with long and short stitch using V. Embroider two highlights in straight stitch with U, and the apple stem in straight stitch using P. Change to E and work two detached chains, one inside the other, to form the leaf.

BASKET

Using O, work vertical straight stitches approximately 2mm (¹/₁₆") apart across the front of the basket for the foundation of the needleweaving (*diag 2*).

(diag 2)

Bring the same thread to the front at the top right hand side of the basket. Change to the tapestry needle and weave the thread across the line of vertical stitches, then take it to the back on the left hand side. Bring the thread to the surface just beneath the previous row and weave back across the vertical stitches, alternating the over/under sequence from the first row (*diag 3*).

(diag 3)

Continue working in this manner until the shape is filled. Changing to C, work a line of twisted chain stitch along the upper front edge for the rim. Fill the back section of the basket with vertical satin stitch using the same thread. Stitch the outline of the front and back book cover in split stitch with F (*diag 4*).

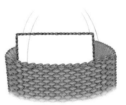

(diag 4)

Fill the front cover of the book with satin stitch using the same thread. Embroider the pages in split stitch with Y. Using two strands of O, stitch the basket handles in twisted chain stitch.

Starting each row at the tip, embroider rows of feather stitch with D for the daisy foliage. Work additional layers of feather stitch with E and AA, slightly off-setting the stitches in each row. For the daisies, stitch the petals with detached chains using Y, and stitch a French knot for each flower centre using K.

BONNET, FACE AND HAIR

Embroider the bonnet in a similar manner to the basket using H. Fan the foundation stitches to fit the shape of the brim and take them over the edge of the felt around the outer edge (*diag 5*).

(diag 5)

Work the weaving in a similar manner to the basket, beginning on the edge closest to the face. Using V, embroider the ribbon ties and bow loops in long and short stitch, and the bow knot in satin stitch. Stitch the knot outline and lower edges of the ribbon tails in stem stitch using B, and the markings on the bow loops in straight stitch with the same thread.

Stitch the hair within the bonnet with long and short stitch using N. Work the skin in long and short stitch with A, and embroider the nose markings, face shaping and neck with straight stitches using X. Work the eyebrows in split stitch with N.

Embroider the remaining face details with straight stitch. Use Z for the cheeks and mouth, Y for the teeth, and V for the mouth highlights. Work the eyes with G and U, and add highlights to the pupils with U.

Work bullion knots for the ringlets using two strands of N. Vary the number of wraps according to the length required to fill the shape. When pushed together on the needle, the number of wraps should match the length of the stitch, plus two wraps.

GRASS

Beginning with D, work fly stitches for the grass. Change to E and work fly stitches and straight stitches over the first layer. Finish the grass by working another layer of fly and straight stitches using AA.

LAMB
BODY AND LEGS

Beginning at the neck, stitch the mid tones of the body shading in long and short stitch using R and S. Fill the remainder of the body and legs in long and short stitch with M. Embroider the knee and hoof markings in straight stitch using G. Work the dark shadows in long and short stitch with T. Change to Y and work straight stitch highlights over the previous stitching across the chest, above each knee and on the rump.

HEAD

Fill the inside of the ears with long and short stitch using S. Work the shading under the chin in split stitch with the same thread. Fill the top of the ears and the face in long and short stitch with M. Embroider the remaining face shading in straight stitch using R and S.

Stitch the eyes in straight stitch using G, and add a straight stitch highlight to each eye with Y.

Embroider the nose and mouth in straight stitch with G. Work the pink inside the ears and around the nose in straight stitch using A. Stitch over the lightest areas of the head in straight stitch using Y.

RIBBON AND BELL

Using I, embroider the ribbon in long and short stitch, completing one section of the tails at a time to define the folds *(diag 6)*.

(diag 6)

Embroider the knot in satin stitch with the same thread. Work the bell in straight stitch using K, and stitch the shading on the bell in straight stitch with T.

GRASS AND DAISIES

Using E, stitch tufts of grass below the lamb in straight stitch. Stitch a second layer using D. Work a final layer of fly and straight stitches with a combination of D, E and AA.

Using two strands of Y, stitch the daisy petals with detached chains. Work the daisy centres in French knots using two strands of K.

LETTERING

Remove the blanket from the hoop.

Embroider the letters in back stitch and add a French knot for each dot using G. Changing to E, work the scrolls for the daisy spray in stem stitch. Embroider the daisy leaves in layers of feather stitch, using E, D and AA, in a similar manner to Mary's basket. Stitch the daisy petals with detached chains using two strands of Y. Add the centres in French knots using two strands of K. Stitch three French knots at the end of each scroll with AA.

Construction

See pages 78–84.

Construction

- See the liftout pattern for templates and cutting out details.

- These instructions apply to all blankets unless otherwise specified.

- All seam allowances are 1cm ($^3/_8$") unless otherwise specified.

- The shaded areas on the construction diagrams indicate the right side of the fabric.

1. PREPARATION

Carefully remove the tacking stitches from the embroidered piece. If the design was transferred using water-soluble stabiliser, trim away the excess stabiliser. Remove any remaining water-soluble stabiliser or fabric marker with a damp sponge.

Place the embroidered piece face down on a well-padded surface and press carefully, avoiding any raised embroidery.

2. ATTACHING THE BACKING

With the wrong side facing up, place the backing on a smooth, flat surface. With the right side facing up, centre the embroidered blanket onto the backing. Starting at the centre and working outwards, smooth the blanket with the palm of your hand and pin the two layers together. Pin widthwise and lengthwise, then along each diagonal *(diag 1)*.

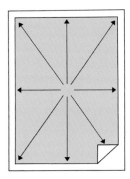

diag 1

Ensure that there are no wrinkles in the backing. Tack along the lines of pins, working from the centre out and removing the pins as you go.

Work lines of tacking 15cm (6") apart along the length of the blanket, then tack around the entire blanket 8cm (3") in from the edge *(diag 2)*.

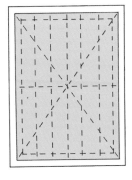

diag 2

Puppy Fun, Wee Willie Winkie and Mary's Little Lamb

Leave the excess backing extending past the edges of the blanket. Use this allowance to form a mitred border on the front of the blanket following the instructions in step 4.

New Life

Trim away any excess backing so that it is even with the raw edge of the blanket.

Machine baste around the edge of the blanket, 12mm (½") in from the raw edge. This will be the stitchline when attaching the binding.

Bind the raw edges following the instructions in step 5.

3. PREPARING SHAPED CORNERS AND EDGING

Blossoms

Trim away any excess backing so that it is even with the raw edge of the blanket. Using the corner template, mark the curves and scallops onto each corner with the fabric marker *(diag 3)*.

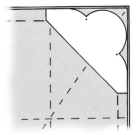

diag 3

On each long side, measure a point 5cm (2") in from the raw edge on the centre line of tacking. Mark this position with a dot for the pivot point. Using the scallop template and matching pivot points, mark the scallop shaping on each long side *(diag 4)*.

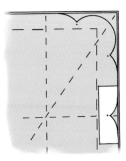

diag 4

Cut out the shaping along the marked lines on all edges. Ensuring the raw edges are matching and the backing fabric is smooth, machine baste around the blanket 12mm (½") in from the raw edge. This will be the stitchline when attaching the binding.

Bundle of Joy

Trim away any excess backing so that it is even with the raw edge of the blanket. Using the corner template, mark the shaping on each corner with the fabric marker *(diag 5)*.

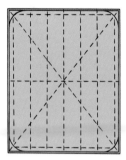

diag 5

Cut the curves along the marked lines. Machine baste around the edge of the blanket 12mm (½") in from the raw edge. This will be the stitchline when attaching the piping and binding.

Starting near one corner, matching raw edges and with right sides facing up, pin the lace edging over the blanket *(diag 6)*.

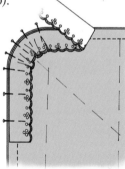

diag 6

Continue pinning around the blanket, easing the edging around the corners. Mark the overlap point on the edging at the starting point. Place the ends of the edging with right sides together. Pin and stitch at the marked position. Trim the excess and press open *(diag 7)*.

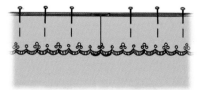

diag 7

Tack the edging in place within the seam allowance.

Starting midway along the lower edge and matching stitchlines, pin the piping in place over the lace edging. At the corners, clip the piping heading and ease the piping around the curves *(diag 8)*.

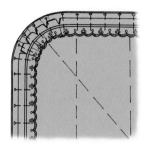

diag 8

Fold the ends of the piping into the seam allowance at the overlap point and trim the excess *(diag 9)*.

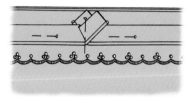

diag 9

Tack the piping in place. Bind the outer edge following the instructions in step 5.

4. ALL-IN-ONE BACKING AND BORDER

If necessary, trim the extending backing to the following measurement on all four edges of the blanket:

Puppy Fun: 7.5cm (3")

Wee Willie Winkie: 6.5cm (2 ½")

Mary's Little Lamb: 10.5cm (4 ⅛")

Puppy Fun and Wee Willie Winkie

With the blanket facing up, fold in and press 1cm (⅜") on all sides of the backing *(diag 10)*.

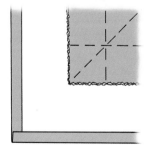

diag 10

Mary's Little Lamb

Fold 5cm (2") of the backing in so that the edge of the backing meets the raw edge of the blanket on all sides (*diag 11*).

diag 11

Puppy Fun, Wee Willie Winkie and Mary's Little Lamb

Fold in and press the remaining backing, so that it fits firmly around the edges of the blanket (*diag 12*).

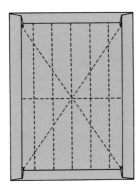

diag 12

Unfold the backing to lay flat on the *Puppy Fun* and *Wee Willie Winkie* blankets. For *Mary's Little Lamb*, leave the first layer of the backing folded.

Diagonally fold in one corner of the backing so that it folds on the exact corner of the blanket. Ensure that the upper left and lower right corners are at a 45 degree angle. Press along the diagonal foldline (*diags 13a & 13b*).

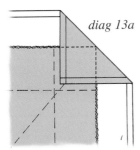
diag 13a

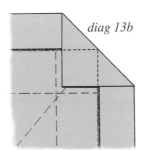
diag 13b

Puppy Fun and
Wee Willlie Winkie

Mary's Little Lamb

Unfold. Repeat for the remaining corners.

PREPARING THE PIPING

Puppy Fun

Cut two lengths of the green piping measuring 70cm (27 ½") and another two lengths measuring 100cm (39 ½"). Repeat for the tan piping. Place one long length of green piping over the tan, abutting the piping. Machine baste together along the stitchline of the green piping (*diag 14*).

diag 14

Repeat with the remaining lengths to form two short and two long lengths of double piping.

Wee Willie Winkie

Cut two lengths of the red gingham piping measuring 67cm (26 ½") and another two lengths measuring 107cm (42").

ATTACHING THE PIPING

Puppy Fun and Wee Willie Winkie

Mark 1cm (⅜") inside each end of the pressed diagonal line on the backing. The ends of the piping will align with these marks (*diag 15*).

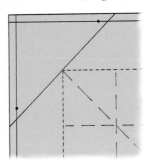

diag 15

Pin and stitch the short lengths of piping to each short side of the backing on the right side, aligning the ends of the piping with the marked points and the piping stitchline with the 1cm (⅜") foldline (*diag 16*).

diag 16

Attach the long lengths to the remaining sides in the same manner.

For *Puppy Fun*, treat the double piping in the same manner as single piping. Position it on the backing with the green piping facing down, and follow the basting line when stitching *(diag 17)*.

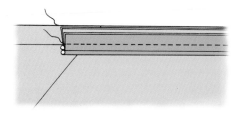

diag 17

Press the piped edges to the wrong side along the foldline, with the piping extending over the edge.

FORMING THE MITRED CORNERS

With right sides together and matching the pressed diagonal foldlines, fold the corner back on itself and pin. Stitch along the diagonal foldline *(diags 18a & 18b)*.

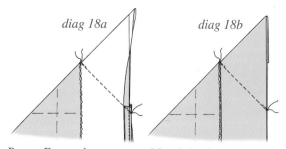

diag 18a   *diag 18b*

Puppy Fun and   *Mary's Little Lamb*
Wee Willlie Winkie

Trim the seam, leaving a 1cm (³⁄₈") seam allowance, and then trim across the corner *(diag 19)*.

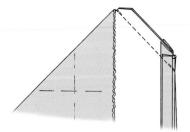

diag 19

Press the seam open. Repeat at the remaining corners.

Turn the corners to the right side, creating a border over the right side of the blanket. Ensure that the blanket sits flat inside each corner.

COMPLETING THE BORDER

Pin the border to the blanket along all sides, ensuring it is an even depth around the blanket. Using sewing thread to match the backing fabric, topstitch the border in place through all layers, stitching close to the folded edge of the border and pivoting at the corners with the needle in the fabric *(diag 20)*.

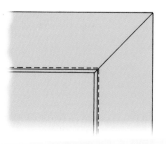

diag 20

FINISHING

Remove all tacking threads from the blanket and carefully press the border.

5. SEPARATE BINDING

Bundle of Joy, New Life and Blossoms

JOINING THE BINDING STRIPS

With right sides together, place the end of one binding strip at right angles over the end of a second strip. Stitch using a 6mm (¹⁄₄") seam allowance *(diag 21)*.

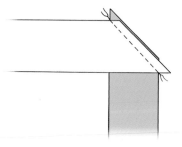

diag 21

Press the seam open. Join all the binding strips in this manner until one length is formed. Fold the binding in half along the length, with wrong sides together, and press.

ATTACHING THE BINDING

Where possible, avoid placing any joins near corners or pivot points when attaching the binding.

Start in the middle of the lower edge, with 8cm (3") of binding extending past the starting point. With right sides together and raw edges even, begin to pin the binding along the edge of the blanket on the right side. Place the pins at right angles to the raw edge *(diag 22)*.

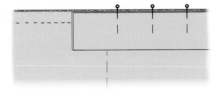

diag 22

New Life

Continue to pin up to the first corner. Beginning the stitching 16cm (6 ¼") from the end of the binding and using a 12mm (½") seam allowance, stitch the binding in place. Finish 1cm (⅜") from the first corner *(diag 23)*.

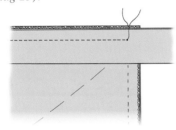

diag 23

Fold the binding upwards to form a 45 degree fold and finger press *(diag 24)*.

diag 24

Holding the fold in place, fold the binding back down along the adjacent side, aligning the raw edges as before. Continue to pin and stitch in place, beginning 1cm (⅜") from the corner *(diag 25)*.

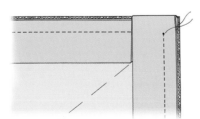

diag 25

Continue attaching the binding around the blanket in this manner, finishing 16cm (6 ¼") from the starting point and leaving 8cm (3") of binding overlapping.

Bundle of Joy

Continue to pin the binding around the blanket, easing it to fit the curves at the corners and finishing with 8cm (3") of binding overlapping at the starting point. Beginning and ending 16cm (6 ½") from the ends of the binding and stitching as close as possible to the corded edge of the piping, stitch the binding in place with a 12mm (½") seam allowance *(diag 26)*.

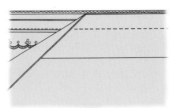

diag 26

Blossoms

Continue to pin the binding up to the first pivot point. Using a 12mm (½") seam allowance, stitch up to the pivot point, ending off the threads securely *(diag 27)*.

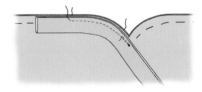

diag 27

Clip the seam allowance almost to the stitchline at the pivot point. Continue pinning and stitching in the same manner until reaching the first corner. At the corner, pin and tack the binding around the curve before machine stitching in place. Continue attaching the binding in the same manner, finishing the stitching 6cm (6 ¼") from the starting point and leaving 8cm (3") of the binding overlapping.

Joining the binding

Lay the ends of the binding side by side and mark each with a pin at the centre point of the overlap *(diag 28)*.

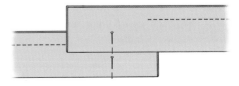

diag 28

Open out the ends of the binding strip and measure a 1cm (³⁄₈") seam allowance beyond the pin marks. Cutting along the straight grain (diagonally across the strip), trim away the excess binding beyond the seam allowance.

With right sides together, place one end at right angles over the other. Stitch at the marked point (diag 29).

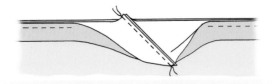

diag 29

Press the seam open. Refold the binding. Pin and stitch the remaining section of binding to the blanket. Press the binding towards the outer edge. Fold the binding to the back of the blanket, enclosing the seam allowance.

COMPLETING THE BINDING

New Life

Working on the back of the blanket, pin the binding so the folded edge meets the previous row of stitching. Shape and pin the corners into mitres as you come to them. Using matching sewing thread, handstitch the binding in place (diag 30).

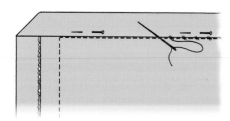

diag 30

Bundle of Joy

Working on the back of the blanket and easing the binding to fit the curves on the corners, pin the binding so that the folded edge meets the previous row of stitching. Using matching sewing thread, handstitch in place.

Blossoms

Working on the back of the blanket and easing the fabric around the scallops, pin the binding so that the folded edge meets the previous row of stitching. Using matching sewing thread, handstitch the binding in place (diag 31).

diag 31

With the right side facing up, place the blanket on a flat surface. At one pivot point, fold the excess binding fabric so a dart is formed at right angles to the point. The excess fabric is inside the layers of binding (diag 32).

diag 32

Stitch the dart with tiny stitches through the fold of the dart and the fabric directly beneath (diag 33).

diag 33

Fold the darts and stitch in the same manner on all the remaining pivot points.

FINISHING

Remove all tacking threads from the blanket and carefully press the binding.

Stitch Glossary

BACK STITCH

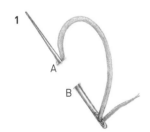

BLANKET STITCH

1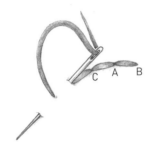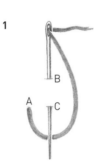

2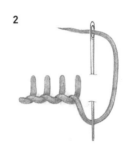

BLANKET STITCH PINWHEEL

1

2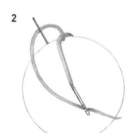

3

BULLION KNOT

1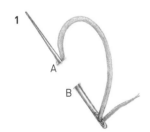

Bring thread to front at A. Pick up fabric the required length of the finished knot.

2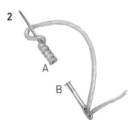

Wind enough wraps around the needle to cover required distance.

3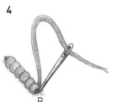

Holding wraps, pull needle through.

4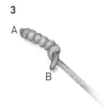

Insert needle at B.

5

BULLION LOOP

A B

A loop is formed when A and B are very close and many wraps are used.

CHAIN STITCH

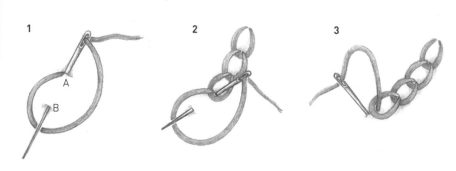

1   A   B

2

3

COLONIAL KNOT

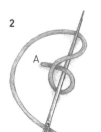

1 A

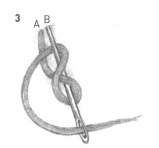

2 A

3 A B

COUCHING

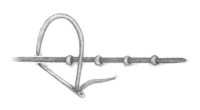

Laid thread is attached using a second thread.

CRESTED CHAIN STITCH

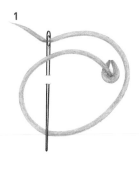

1

2

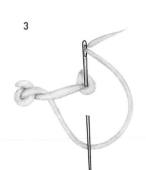

3

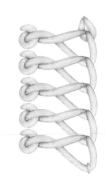

4

CROSS STITCH

DETACHED CHAIN

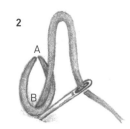

1 A B

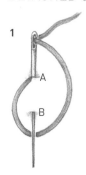

2 A B

3

FEATHER STITCH

1 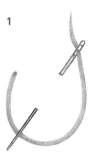 **2** 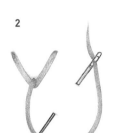 **3** 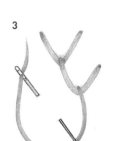 **4**

FLY STITCH

1  **2** 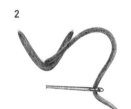 **3**

FRENCH KNOT

1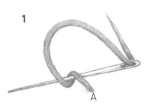

2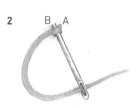

3

GHIORDES KNOT

1  **2** 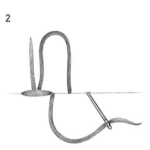 **3**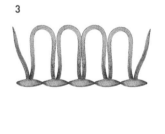

4  **5**

GRANITOS

1

2

3

LONG AND SHORT STITCH

1

2

3

PADDED SATIN STITCH

1 – satin stitch

2 – split stitch

3 – seed stitch

RAISED CROSS STITCH FLOWER

1
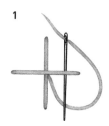

2
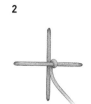

3

4

SEED STITCH

1

2

RUNNING STITCH

1
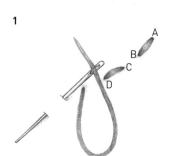

SATIN STITCH

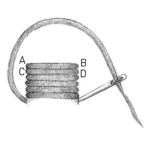

SIDE RIBBON STITCH

left

right

SMOCKER'S KNOT

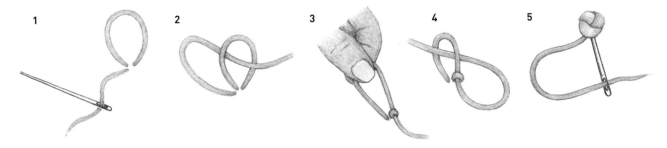

1   2   3   4   5

SPLIT BACK STITCH

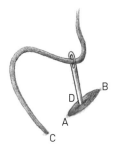

SPLIT STITCH

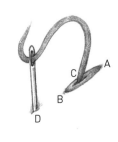

STEM STITCH

The thread is always kept below the needle.

WHIPPING

1 – over back stitch

2 – over couched stitch

TWISTED CHAIN STITCH

1

2

End off in the same manner as chain stitch

TWISTED DETACHED CHAIN

1

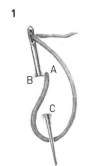

2

WHIPPED REVERSE CHAIN STITCH

1   2

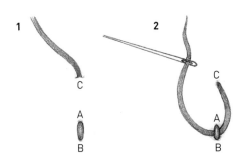

3

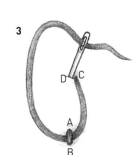

4

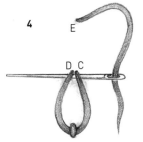

5

Country Bumpkin Classics

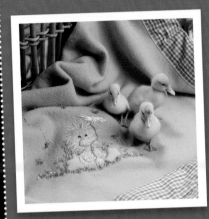

The Duckling

Fruits of the Hedgerow

Petit Amour

Rock A Bye Baby

The Great Escape

The Loved Ones

The Woolly Sheep

Creature Comforts

Toy Soldiers

Arabian Nights

Make Believe

Midnight Feast

Windflower

Schererezade

Market Day

Bunny Love

Forget-Me-Not

Now be even more inspired...

INSPIRATIONS Magazine

Published in Australia, *Inspirations* is loved by readers across the world. Each issue includes original designs and quality patterns using a range of traditional and modern techniques. Clear instructions and fully illustrated step-by-step stitch guides make the magazine perfect for beginner and experienced stitchers alike.

You'll also find pages filled with embroidery news, information on the latest products and books, and fascinating needlework stories from around the world.

Contact us to find out how to get hold of a copy today!

A-Z Series

The ultimate reference series for embroiderers, each book features a comprehensive collection of clearly photographed step-by-step stitches. Filled with informative hints and techniques, these practical, easy-to-follow books are suitable for beginner and advanced stitchers alike.

A-Z of Embroidery Stitches

A-Z of Embroidery Stitches 2

A-Z of Wool Embroidery

INSPIRATIONS Index

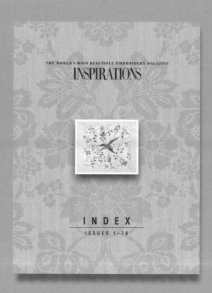

A complete guide to **INSPIRATIONS issues 1–76 featuring:**

- Comprehensive listings including designer and description
- Alphabetical listing of step-by-steps
- Detailed general index
- All known errata

An indispensable resource for evey *Inspirations* lover!